The Life of Jesus Christ

The Life of Jesus Christ

Understanding the Story of the Gospels

Russell Shaw

Our Sunday Visitor
Huntington, Indiana

Nihil Obstat
Msgr. Michael Heintz, Ph.D.
Censor Librorum

Imprimatur
✠ Kevin C. Rhoades
Bishop of Fort Wayne-South Bend
June 12, 2021

26 25 24 23 22 21   1 2 3 4 5 6 7 8 9

Our Sunday Visitor Publishing Division
Our Sunday Visitor, Inc.
200 Noll Plaza
Huntington, IN 46750
1-800-348-2440

ISBN: 978-1-68192-425-0 (Inventory No. T2568)
1. RELIGION—Christian Theology—Christology.
2. RELIGION—Christianity—Catholic.
3. RELIGION—Christianity—History.
eISBN: 978-1-68192-426-7
LCCN: 2021937935

Cover and interior design: Lindsey Riesen
Cover art: Detail of Jesus Christ from the painting, *Christ and the Rich Young Ruler* by H. Hofmann, Restored Traditions

Printed in the United States of America

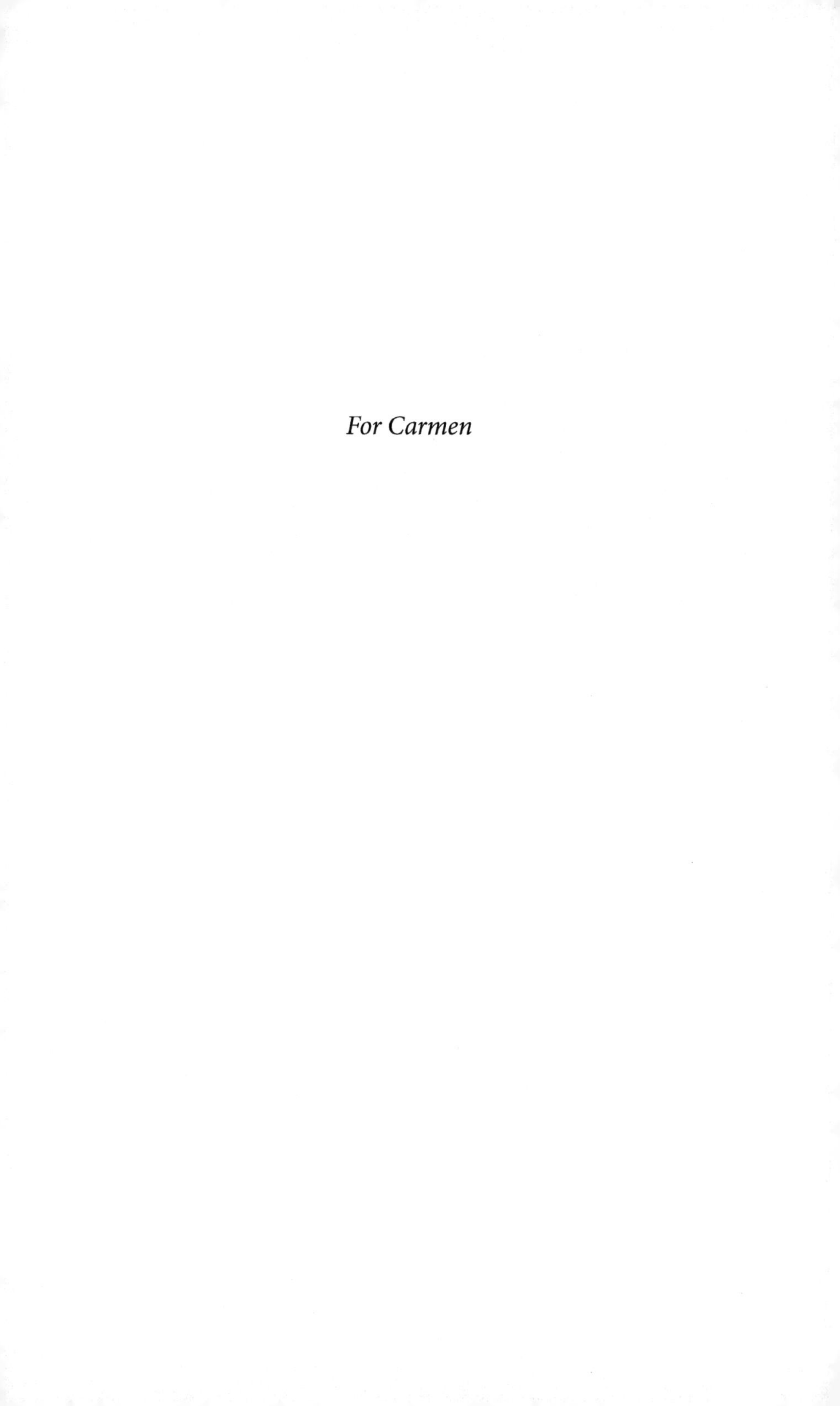

For Carmen

CONTENTS

Introduction

When receiving an Emmy for his TV show "Life Is Worth Living" in 1952, Bishop Fulton Sheen made it a point to include in his acceptance remarks "special thanks to my writers — Matthew, Mark, Luke, and John." I'm no Fulton Sheen, but I can say the same thing concerning this book: Sincere thanks to the four evangelists for supplying the material.

In my own life, long after Bishop Sheen got his Emmy, something happened that helps to explain how this book came to be. My wife and I belonged to a Catholic couples' group whose members met monthly to share a potluck meal and discuss a topic of a spiritual nature. That year's topic was the Gospel of Matthew. Month by month, we worked our way through it, reading and discussing a chapter or two at a time.

Gathering as usual one month at the home of one of the couples, we shared an enjoyable meal, then adjourned to the living room for the discussion. It was the custom to take turns leading the discussion. This particular month, it was the turn of one of the other husbands. Our leader — a highly educated man who was a lifelong practicing Catholic — began by announcing that, out of curiosity, he'd read the whole of Matthew's Gospel straight through from beginning to end. Then he made a surprising admission: This was the first time he'd ever read one of the Gospels that way. He paused to let that sink in, then said: "And you know what?" Another pause. Then, in the manner of someone disclosing an exciting discovery: "*It's telling a story!*"

Our friend went on to explain that, every Sunday at Mass, he heard a short passage from one of the Gospels read — a bit of instruction this week, a miracle or parable next week — and on and on, week by week, a stream of seemingly unrelated snippets. Unless the priest happened to mention it in his homily (and most did not), there was never a hint concerning how this week's snippet related to last week's or next week's snippets, much less how the day's passage fit into the Gospel narrative as a whole. For that, you needed to do as he'd just done — read the Gospel all the way through. And if you did that, you would learn what he learned:

"*It's telling a story!*"

And so it is. The story that the Gospels tell is the life of Jesus Christ.

Thinking about that incident since then, something else has occurred to me. By itself, any particular Gospel tells only some of the story of Jesus of Nazareth. True, each Gospel contains a special, precious portion, but no one Gospel by itself contains the whole of it. And not only that — although the Gospels of Matthew, Mark, and Luke follow pretty much the same pattern in recounting Christ's life, the Gospel of John is strikingly different and contains a great deal of material found nowhere else. So, to get the whole story of Jesus as the four Gospels together tell it, you have to combine elements from each of them into a single, coherent narrative.

Which, roughly, is this book's goal.

In a way, there's nothing new about that. "Harmonies" of the Gospels, as they're called, have been composed for a long time. One of the earliest of these, the work of a man named Tatian in the second century, was widely used by Christians in some places for several centuries.

Unfortunately, though, Tatian had the notion that his harmonized version could and should be read in place of the four individual Gospels themselves. Let me say as clearly as I can that the present book is not meant to substitute for reading the Gospels, but to help readers grasp the story told by the four of them. I hope that, in doing this, the book will be helpful not only to people who may be coming to the Gospels for the first time, but also to those who've been familiar with them for many years and would like to have their story assembled in one place.

Please note, though — this isn't a fictionalized treatment of the life of Christ like Fulton Oursler's hugely popular 1950s bestseller *The Greatest Story Ever Told.* This book sticks closely to the Gospels, with only such commentary and explanation as may help make their meaning clearer. Limitations of space made it necessary to omit many important passages found in the originals, which is all the more reason not to stop here, but to go on to read and reflect on the Gospels themselves.

Modern scholarship sheds much useful light on the origins of the Gospels, but it's as true now as it has always been that these inspired accounts, in the words of the Second Vatican Council, "faithfully hand on what Jesus, the Son of God … really did and taught." I pray this book will help readers understand and appreciate the wonderful story the four Gospels tell.

Of course, merely reading about Jesus is not enough. We need to become acquainted with Jesus himself, and that can only happen by thinking about him, considering his words and deeds in our minds, and especially seeking him in prayer and worship. As Monsignor Romano Guardini, the distinguished theologian whom I will quote frequently, says about getting to know Jesus: "We must follow him. We must strive to penetrate into the heart of his mystery, to what he really is. Then things become plain."

Books alone will not accomplish that, but books are a help. And the Gospels of Matthew, Mark, Luke, and John are the greatest help of all. Finally, then, there is no better way to conclude this introduction to the story of Jesus as the evangelists tell it than these words from the Gospel of Saint John: "Now Jesus did many other signs in the presence of his disciples, which are not written in this book; but these are written that you may believe that Jesus is the Christ, the Son of God, and that believing you may have life in his name" (Jn 20:30–31).

Russell Shaw

1
Beginnings

There is no finer introduction to the life of Jesus Christ than the soaring, poignant prologue of the Gospel of Saint John:

"In the beginning was the Word, and the Word was with God, and the Word was God. He was in the beginning with God; all things were made through him, and without him was not anything made that was made. In him was life, and the life was the light of men. The light shines in the darkness, and the darkness has not overcome it.

"There was a man sent from God, whose name was John. He came for testimony, to bear witness to the light, that all might believe through him. He was not the light, but came to bear witness to the light.

"The true light that enlightens every man was coming into the world. He was in the world, and the world was made through him, yet the world knew him not. He came to his own home, and his own people received him not. But to all who received him, who believed in his name, he gave power to become children of God; who were born, not of blood nor of the will of the flesh nor of the will of man, but of God.

"And the Word became flesh and dwelt among us, full of grace and truth; we have beheld his glory, glory as of the only-begotten Son from the Father. ... And from his fulness have we all received, grace upon grace."

Although they differ in many particulars, the Gospels of Matthew, Mark, and Luke all give similar accounts of Jesus' life; they are called the "Synoptic" Gospels since they share the same general viewpoint. But John's Gospel is unlike the others because it has a different source — the recollections of the beloved disciple, as Saint John is called in the Gospel that bears his name. All of the Gospels are precious sources of information; despite their differences, the same commanding figure, that of Jesus Christ, stands at the center of all four.

The Gospels according to Saint Matthew and Saint Luke contain genealogies of Jesus, in their first and third chapters, respectively. The two lists of names are quite different, but they agree in placing Jesus in the line of notable Old Testament figures. They deliver a pointed reminder that Jesus himself was the fulfillment of the Old Covenant's Messianic promises, yet they acknowledge that he came to inaugurate a New Covenant between God and humanity. The genealogies also are careful to establish Jesus' link to King David through his foster father, Joseph — a matter of great importance to identifying him as Messiah in the eyes of Jewish readers. The Old Testament prophets had foretold that the eagerly awaited Redeemer-King of Israel would belong to the Davidic line.

Zechariah and the Angel

The narrative opens (in Luke's Gospel) with an elderly Jewish priest named Zechariah. He and his wife, Elizabeth, were pious people living with a heavy disappointment: After many years of marriage, they had no offspring and had abandoned hope of having any, since Zechariah was old and Elizabeth was past childbearing age.

At times, Zechariah was called on to serve in the great Temple in Jerusalem, the heart and center of Jewish religious life. Many years earlier, the reigning king, Herod the Great, had undertaken a major expansion and renovation of this vast structure to ingratiate himself with his subjects. Although the Temple project failed to increase the popularity of this cruel ruler — a non-Jew who owed his kingship to the Roman occupiers of Palestine — the Jews were nevertheless immensely proud of the imposing edifice that, as we shall see, was to be the site of many crucial events in Jesus' life.

One day, Zechariah had the task of performing the afternoon ritual — offering incense in the Holy Place, which was the second most sacred section of the entire Temple. While the people prayed outside, the old man entered the chamber alone and began the rite. But then he froze: Standing there, next to the altar, was an angel — no less than the Archangel Gabriel himself, as Zechariah would learn.

Zechariah was understandably terrified; but his heavenly visitor spoke soothing words, reassuring him, "Do not be afraid. Your prayer is heard, and your wife Elizabeth will bear you a son, and you shall call his name John." Not only that — this unexpected child would grow up to resemble the great prophet Elijah himself as forerunner of God's Anointed One, the Messiah, preaching a message of repentance and conversion to the people.

Zechariah listened in astonishment as the archangel spoke, but now he made a mistake. In the course of a long life, he'd experienced his share of unkept promises and disappointed hopes, and those painful memories now led him to ask, considering the circumstances, an impertinent question: "How shall I know this?" In other words, what sign would prove that these remarkable things would really come to pass?

The archangel was not pleased. Zechariah would get his sign, but not the sort of sign that he expected. "I am Gabriel, who stand in the presence of God," he declared sternly, "and I was sent to speak to you, and to bring you this good news. And behold, you will be silent and unable to speak until the day when these things come to pass, because you did not believe my words."

And with that, Gabriel was gone. Pulling himself together as best he could, Zechariah stumbled out of the Holy Place, speechless and wild-eyed — looking very much as a man who'd just seen an archangel might be expected to look. When his Temple service ended, he returned to his wife, Elizabeth, and their home in the Judean hill country, a town called Ein Kerem. And soon, just as Gabriel had said, Elizabeth conceived a child and went into seclusion to await the birth.

The Annunciation

Elizabeth was six months pregnant when God dispatched Gabriel to deliver another message, this time to a young Jewish woman in a town called Nazareth, which was tucked away in an isolated corner of the province of Galilee. At that time, neither Galilee nor Nazareth was considered significant by the Jews of Judea and Jerusalem. Galilee was considered a place where the local Jews mixed all too freely with Romans and other pagans, while Nazareth, lying in a valley cut off from the world by the surrounding hills, was the butt of a proverbial joke: "Can anything good come out of Nazareth?" Hometown of the Messiah? Certainly not! When the Messiah came, it would surely not be from there.

The young woman's name was Mariam — Mary. Tradition identifies her parents as Joachim and Ann. At this time, she was probably about fifteen, hardly more than a child by present standards, but of marriageable age in those days. She was wholly unknown to anyone but her family and her immediate circle of friends and neighbors. They likely considered her a sweet, deeply religious girl, but also a bit of a dreamer. As we now know, however, she was an extraordinary individual with an extraordinary role in God's redemptive plan. And what the Gospels tell us about her makes it clear that she was intelligent, prayerful, modest, resolute, and entirely open to God's will.

All of that was apparent in her dialogue with Gabriel and the startling words with which he addressed her: "Hail, full of grace, the Lord is with you!"

Her first reaction, very likely, was wonderment: What could that possibly mean? Seeing she was puzzled, the archangel went on quickly: "Do not be afraid, Mary, for you have found favor with God. And behold, you will conceive in your womb and bear a son, and you shall call his name Jesus." Furthermore, this son of hers would do remarkable things: "He will be great, and will be called the Son of the Most High; and the Lord God will give him the throne of his father David, and he will reign over the house of Jacob forever; and of his kingdom there will be no end."

Mary was still uncertain. Although she was betrothed to Joseph, a carpenter whose ancestry extended back to the great King David himself, it appears that she had quietly committed herself to perpetual virginity as an expression of total commitment to God, and that she and Joseph had agreed to practice continence in their marriage. Quite reasonably, therefore, she now asked a question: "How will this be, since I do not know man?"

While Zechariah was punished when he asked a question, Mary's question was to be rewarded with a breath-taking answer. But the two questions were fundamentally different. Zechariah's expressed skepticism regarding what he'd been told, but Mary's was a straightforward, eminently practical request for information: What should she do to comply with God's will for her?

And Gabriel had a ready answer: "The Holy Spirit will come upon you, and the power of the Most High will overshadow you; therefore the child to be born will be called holy, the Son of God." Then he shared surprising news: Her cousin Elizabeth, supposedly too old to have a child, was now six months pregnant. "For with God nothing will be impossible."

Theologian Romano Guardini speaks admiringly of the royal character of Mary's response. Facing a divine request to do something "far beyond human comprehension," he remarks, she answered simply and with profound dignity, "utterly unconscious of the greatness of her act."

"Behold," she said, "I am the handmaid of the Lord; let it be to me according to your word."

Mission accomplished, Gabriel left her. And Mary quickly set about making arrangements to visit Elizabeth and join her in marveling at the divine plan now unfolding, whereby God had reached out to the two of them and made them part of his great project.

The Visitation

Ein Kerem, the town near Jerusalem where Zechariah and Elizabeth lived, was several days' journey from Nazareth. Almost certainly, Mary did not go alone. Did Joseph accompany her? The Gospels don't say. Perhaps he did, or she may have joined pilgrims on their way to Jerusalem for Passover, or a caravan of merchants headed in that direction. In any case, the southward trek — seventy miles or so — would have occupied three or four days. It's safe to assume she made good use of the time, thinking and praying about God's mysterious will in these events.

Upon reaching her destination, Mary greeted her cousin warmly, and as she did, Elizabeth's own child leaped in her womb. Elizabeth, with the Spirit of prophecy upon her, burst out joyfully: "Blessed are you among women, and blessed is the fruit of your womb." Mary responded with a glowing hymn of praise and gratitude to God that drew upon the sacred texts of Israel that she knew so well. Today, we know Mary's hymn as the Magnificat:

"My soul magnifies the Lord, and my spirit rejoices in God my Savior, for he has regarded the low estate of his handmaiden. For behold, henceforth all generations will call me blessed; for he who is mighty has done great things for me, and holy is his name. And his mercy is on those who fear him from generation to generation.

"He has shown strength with his arm, he has scattered the proud in the imagination of their hearts, he has put down the mighty from their thrones, and exalted those of low degree; he has filled the hungry with good things, and the rich he has sent empty away. He has helped his servant Israel, in remembrance of his mercy, as he spoke to our fathers, to Abraham and to his posterity for ever."

Mary remained with Elizabeth until near the time Elizabeth would give birth. Then she returned to Nazareth to await the birth of her own son.

About Joseph

Mary told Joseph that she was expecting a child and likely told him something of the circumstances. Joseph, a man of great modesty and delicacy, drew the self-effacing conclusion that here were great matters far beyond him. Intending to spare Mary humiliation, he therefore decided to put her aside privately, as Jewish law permitted him to do. But he had a dream in which an angel told him not to draw back from taking Mary as his wife, "for that which is conceived in her is of the Holy Spirit; she will bear a son, and you shall call his name Jesus, for he will save his people from their sins."

Joseph did as the angel said. He took Mary as his wife, gave the child the name the angel had announced, made a home for the three of them, and served as Jesus' foster father. The New Testament does not record any words from Joseph, and that has led some people to call him Joseph the Silent. But from what the Gospels do tell us, we know many things about him, and especially the most important thing: He was a "just" man. This is great praise in biblical language; to be just meant that he possessed high character and deep piety. Pope St. John Paul II sums up his special role in the drama of salvation like this: "What Joseph did united him in an altogether special way to the faith of Mary. He accepted as truth coming from God the very thing that she had already accepted at the Annunciation. … Therefore he became a unique guardian of the mystery 'hidden for ages in God' (Eph 3:9)."

The Birth of John the Baptist

Elizabeth's son was born soon after Mary returned to Nazareth. On the eighth day after his birth, family and friends gathered for the infant's circumcision and naming. Everyone supposed he would be named Zechariah after his father. But Elizabeth said no — "he shall be called John." The visitors turned to Zechariah and asked him his preference. Still mute, the old priest took a writing tablet and wrote, "His name is John." And at once his speech was restored, while all present marveled.

Word of these happenings spread rapidly throughout the Judean hill country. "What will this child be?" people asked. Zechariah uttered a prophecy now, filled with the Holy Spirit, as Elizabeth had been months earlier. Like Mary's Magnificat, his words brimmed with Old Testament resonances, together with confident faith that the deliverance from enemies promised by God to Israel was finally at hand:

"Blessed be the Lord God of Israel, for he has visited and redeemed his people, and has raised up a horn of salvation for us in the house of his servant David, as he spoke by the mouth of his holy prophets from of old, that we should be saved from our enemies, and from the hand of all who hate us; to perform the mercy promised to our fathers, and to remember his holy covenant, the oath which he swore to our father Abraham, to grant us that we, being delivered from the hand of our enemies, might serve him without fear, in holiness and righteousness before him all the days of our life.

"And you, child, will be called the prophet of the Most High;

for you will go before the Lord to prepare his ways, to give knowledge of salvation to his people in the forgiveness of their sins, through the tender mercy of our God, when the day shall dawn upon us from on high to give light to those who sat in darkness and in the shadow of death, to guide our feet into the way of peace."

This child grew, becoming the man known to us as John the Baptist. Some people speculate that John may have spent time in formation among the Essenes, an ascetical, celibate Jewish monastic sect (best known today as the source of the Dead Sea Scrolls) whose teachings in some ways foreshadowed Christianity. Since the New Testament says nothing about the Essenes, others speculate that they disappeared from the pages of history after becoming early members of the Christian community. Whatever happened, we know for certain that when the time appointed by God came, John went out into the desert to baptize and preach as herald of the Messiah.

SCRIPTURE

John 1:1–14
Matthew 1:1–16
Luke 1:5–80; 3:23–38

2

Nativity and Hidden Years

"In those days," Luke's Gospel recalls, "a decree went out from Caesar Augustus that all the world should be enrolled." And so began the series of events immediately preceding the birth of Jesus Christ, a birth that marked the entrance of the Second Person of the Trinity into human history and acted as the first scene in the climax of God's great redemptive drama.

This entrance could hardly have been more modest and reserved.

Luke is our principal source of information about what happened. According to long tradition, he heard the story from the Blessed Virgin herself. The census commanded by the Roman emperor required that Jewish men register at their ancestral cities and towns. Thus, Joseph, as a descendant of King David, had to go to Bethlehem, the village near Jerusalem from which David himself had come. Joseph traveled with Mary, his betrothed wife, who by now was well along in pregnancy.

This seems strange at first, even rash. What could Joseph possibly have been thinking to subject his young wife to the rigors of a physically taxing journey, so close to the child's birth? The Gospels don't say, but here is a guess.

As a pious Jew, Mary would have known the passage in the Old Testament Book of Micah that says the Messiah, like his great forebear King David, would come from Bethlehem: "But you, O Bethlehem Ephrathah, who are little to be among the clans of Judah, from you shall come forth for me one who is to be ruler in Israel, whose origin is from of old, from ancient days." Mary also knew, or at least strongly suspected, that her child, whose great destiny had been disclosed to her by the archangel Gabriel, was himself the Redeemer. She had wondered, without anxiety, how God would arrange for her to be in Bethlehem when the time came for the child to be born. Now, here was the answer: Yahweh had seen to it that this Roman emperor, without knowing or intending it, should supply what was required.

Mary explained to Joseph why she needed to go with him to Bethlehem to give birth, and he, faithful as always to God's will as it was made known to him, agreed.

The Birth of Jesus

The accounts of Jesus' birth given in the Gospels of Luke and Matthew challenge our conventional expectations for such a momentous event. Why would the Creator and Lord of the world enter it now in obscurity and poverty — "taking the form of a servant," as Saint Paul says? But is this really a surprise? Would Jesus' birth have been more significant in a palace? How could the Son of God become also Son of Man, except in a manner befitting the humility of one who had come "not to be served but to serve, and to give his life as a ransom for many"?

And so, Mary and Joseph went to Bethlehem. "And while they were there, the time came for her to be delivered. And she gave birth to her first-born son and wrapped him in swaddling cloths, and laid him in a manger, because there was no place for them in the inn."

That night, shepherds were watching their sheep in the fields outside Bethlehem. They were men of a rough-and-ready breed, living on the fringes of society. But God, again reversing conventional values, chose rough fellows to hear the good news first. An angel appeared to the shepherds and announced, "To you is born this day in the city of David a Savior, who is Christ the Lord." And suddenly a multitude of angels filled the heavens singing, "Glory to God in the highest, and on earth peace among men with whom he is pleased."

Hurrying to Bethlehem, the shepherds found the child lying in a manger as the angel had said, and there they paid him homage. Then they returned to their sheep, praising God for what they had seen and heard. Mary, reflective as always, thought and prayed over everything.

The exact date of Jesus' birth is unknown, but a reasonable calculation places it in 7 or 6 B.C. We know from the Gospels that it happened not long before the death of Herod the Great in 4 B.C. That Jesus was born "Before Christ" simply reflects a mistake in dating by the compilers of our present calendar. The Prince of Peace came into a world of deep-seated tensions and animosities. True, the Romans had imposed peace (of a sort) on Palestine. But around the time of Jesus' birth, a hothead named Judas the Galilean led a revolt against the Romans that was put down with many casualties. The legacy of that uprising was a party of would-be insurrectionists called Zealots, one or perhaps two of whom — Simon the Zealot and, possibly, Judas Iscariot — would be numbered years later among Jesus' apostles.

Eight days after his birth, the child was circumcised and named Jesus, the name given to Mary by the archangel Gabriel and to Joseph by an angel in a dream. Yeshua, a common Jewish name at that time, means "Yahweh Saves," and indicated the mission that, as events would show, this particular Jesus had come into the world to accomplish.

Forty days after the Nativity, Mary and Joseph went to the Temple in nearby Jerusalem for her purification and the ritual dedication of Jesus to the Lord. An old man named Simeon approached them — "righteous and devout," Luke says of him, and one who was waiting faithfully for Israel's redemption. Moved by the Holy Spirit, Simeon took the child in his arms and prayed fervently, "Lord, now let your servant depart in peace, according to your word; for my eyes have seen your salvation, which you have prepared in the presence of all peoples, a light for revelation to the Gentiles, and for glory to your people Israel." Then, having blessed Joseph and Mary, Simeon spoke directly to the mother: "Behold, this child is set for the fall and rising of many in Israel, and for a sign that is spoken against — and a sword will pierce through your own soul also — that thoughts out of many hearts may be revealed."

They were still in the Temple when an old woman named Anna, a widow and a prophetess, also appeared and, giving thanks to God, assured the bystanders that Jerusalem's redemption had come at last.

The Magi and the Holy Innocents

While the Holy Family was in Bethlehem, unexpected visitors arrived: Magi — learned men from the east (perhaps Persia) — who had come to pay tribute to the newborn king. They explained that the prophetic words of the Old Testament regarding a great King of the Jews, along with a bright heavenly body that they took for a new star, had guided them to Bethlehem.

Tradition tells us the Magi were named Melchior, Caspar, and Balthazar. Today, we would call them astrologers. Sensible people now do not take astrology seriously, but in those days savants like these men searched the heavens as an important source of knowledge; G. K. Chesterton says the Magi represent all those who seek "the truth of things." Clearly, they were men of influence and decent wealth, as they brought Jesus costly gifts: gold representing kingship, incense used in worship, and myrrh, the ointment that would be used to prepare his body for burial years later.

Before reaching Bethlehem, the Magi had stopped in Jerusalem to greet King Herod, and during that visit they ingenuously told Herod that they were seeking the newborn Jewish king. Herod, fearing a threat to his reign, expressed great interest in this news. "Go and search diligently for the child," he told his visitors, "and when you have found him bring me word, that I too may go and worship him." Of course, Herod truly intended not worship, but murder.

Now, having reached Bethlehem and seen Jesus, the Magi were warned in a dream to steer clear of Herod. Bypassing Jerusalem, they therefore headed home by a different route. Meanwhile, an angel appeared to Joseph — also in a dream — and told him, "Take the child and his mother, and flee to Egypt." And so they did. With a Jewish audience in view, Matthew's Gospel is often at pains to note the fulfillment of Old Testament prophecies in the events of Jesus' life, and here Matthew cites the prophet Hosea: "Out of Egypt I have called my son."

When Herod learned that the Magi had tricked him, the furious old king ordered the killing of all male infants and children in and around Bethlehem up to two years old. Estimates place their number at a dozen or so. This may sound like an unimaginable slaughter today, but, in those days, such atrocities were not uncommon. Herod was a notably bloodthirsty king who killed his favorite wife and three of his sons on suspicion of plotting against him. Incidentally, to please his Jewish subjects, Herod, a non-Jew, abstained from pork; the Emperor Caesar Augustus once remarked, while signing the required authorization for Herod to execute one of his sons, "Better to be Herod's pig than his son." Regarding the killing of Bethlehem's innocents, Matthew again quotes an Old Testament prophet, Jeremiah: "A voice was heard in Ramah, wailing and loud lamentation, Rachel weeping for her children; she refused to be consoled, because they were no more." The Church now honors these anonymous little ones as martyrs on the feast of the Holy Innocents, celebrated three days after Christmas.

The Holy Family stayed in Egypt relatively briefly. As we have seen, Herod the Great died in 4 B.C., and after his death Joseph was told in a dream to return to Palestine. But there Joseph learned that Herod's son, Archelaus, had succeeded his father. The son was no less brutal than the father, but less politically astute; a few years later, the Roman emperor, having had enough of him, would send Archelaus into exile in Gaul. But that was in the future. Now, for safety's sake, Joseph took Jesus and Mary back to Galilee, to that remote town called Nazareth.

The Hidden Life

Then began Christ's so-called "hidden life" — the thirty or so years in which he largely disappeared from our sight. Even so, we know a good deal about the circumstances in which he grew to manhood.

Clearly, his mother and foster father were powerful influences. Jesus must have had a physical resemblance to Mary. We know from the Gospels that he resembled her in temperament and mind — intelligent, quick to learn, reflective, sensitive, eager to help others, and above all deeply religious, with an ardent love for his heavenly Father. Furthermore, as Saint Josemaría Escrivá remarks, he must also have resembled Joseph "in his way of working, in the features of his character, in his way of speaking, his realism, his eye for detail, the way he sat at table and broke bread, his preference for using everyday situations to give doctrine."

Like most families in Nazareth, the Holy Family was poor

by today's reckoning. But their poverty was not destitution, and they lived comfortably enough by the modest standards of that time and place. As the town's carpenter, Joseph had a not unimportant role in the economic and social life of Nazareth — being the craftsman everyone went to for projects that ranged from repairing a broken plow to installing beams in a new house. Jesus learned the trade from his foster father. There is an echo of the carpenter's workshop in one of his sayings: "First take the log out of your own eye, and then you will see clearly to take out the speck that is in your brother's eye."

Jesus was brought up in the manner typical of devout, conservative Jews. Besides the day-in, day-out informal tutoring that he received at home from Mary and Joseph, he studied the sacred texts of Israel in the local schoolhouse, the *Beth ha-Sefer.* He became steeped in their wisdom, familiar with Jewish history and traditions, and filled with zeal for the central role in redemption that Yahweh intended for his Chosen People.

All this is clear from the single incident of Jesus' boyhood that we find in Luke's Gospel.

When Jesus was twelve, he accompanied his parents to Jerusalem for the Passover, the greatest feast of the year, which commemorated the Jews' liberation from bondage in Egypt. Thousands of pilgrims flocked to the Holy City to be present for the solemn Temple ceremonies that extended over several days. This year, when the feast was over, Mary and Joseph joined the caravan of friends and family members heading back to Galilee — Mary with the women, Joseph with the men. Each naturally supposed Jesus was with the other, and they had gone a day's journey before realizing that he was not in the caravan.

Back to Jerusalem they rushed to look for him. On the third day, they found him in the Temple, listening to the learned scribes, eagerly asking and answering questions. "All who heard him were amazed at his understanding and his answers," Luke writes.

"Son, why have you treated us so?" Mary asked.

"Did you not know that I must be in my Father's house?" Jesus replied.

Without protest, he returned with them to Nazareth, and there, "obedient to them," resumed his quiet, externally uneventful life, while Mary "kept all these things in her heart."

In his little volume on the Gospels' Infancy Narratives covering the birth and childhood of Christ, Pope Benedict XVI calls attention to Jesus' explanation — "I must be in my Father's house" — of why he remained behind in the Temple. This "must," Pope Benedict points out, is the word used all through the Gospels "whenever mention is made of Jesus' readiness to submit to God's will." Still, he adds, here, as they so often do, Jesus' words "exceed our rational powers," proceed from a realm outside our experience, and require that we respond as his mother did: "Mary does not understand Jesus' saying, but she keeps it in her heart and allows it gradually to come to maturity there."

The years that followed seem to have passed without incident, while "Jesus increased in wisdom and in stature, and in favor with God and man." Hidden years they were, but, as the *Catechism of the Catholic Church* reminds us, by prayerfully imagining what they must have been like, we can "enter into fellowship with Jesus by the most ordinary events of daily life" (533).

Scripture

Matthew 2:1–23
Luke 2:1–52
Philippians 2:5–8
Micah 5:2
Jeremiah 31:15

3

Baptism and Temptation

In Jesus' time, as in ours, Palestine was a hotbed of political, ethnic, and religious tensions. The Romans imposed burdensome taxes and ruled through non-Jewish puppet kings, which chafed painfully on Jewish sensibilities and fed dreams of independence. Messianic longings blended with nationalistic ambitions, creating expectations of a military liberator — God's Anointed One, the Christ — who would lead Israel to glorious victory over the Romans and empower the Chosen People once more in the secular realm.

Into this seething cauldron came a striking, unusual figure — John the Baptist, son of Zechariah and Elizabeth, and cousin of Jesus of Nazareth. Today, we look for our preachers to be neatly combed and conservatively garbed, but people then had different expectations and tastes. Dressed in camel's hair with a broad leather belt around his waist, and subsisting on a diet of locusts and honey, John drew eager crowds from Jerusalem. Those who came sought baptism in the Jordan River and listened avidly to John's message to prepare for the one who was coming — a message directed not only to tax collectors and soldiers, but also to Pharisees and Sadducees, whom he assailed as "vipers."

John was the last in that line of remarkable figures, the Old Testament prophets, whose troubled fate is summed up by Romano Guardini: "now elevated to the summits of power and illumination, now flung back into impotency and darkness, according to the Spirit's will." Later Jesus would call the Baptist "Elijah who is to come," referring to that mighty man of God who had been carried to heaven in a fiery chariot and who, according to the prophet Malachi, would return one day to herald "the great and terrible day of the Lord." Although John's fame and influence were now at their height, he knew very well that his role in God's plan would not last long. "I baptize you with water for repentance," he told his listeners, "but he who is coming after me is mightier than I, whose sandals I am not worthy to carry; he will baptize you with the Holy Spirit and with fire."

The Baptism of Jesus

One day Jesus did come and, to John's chagrin, asked to be baptized. Although not a sacrament, John's baptism was a sign of turning away from sin for those who received it. Jesus was hardly in need of conversion, so John demurred: "I need to be baptized by you, and do you come to me?" But Jesus insisted, so John could only comply. As Jesus rose from the baptismal water, "the heavens were opened and he saw the Spirit of God descending like a dove, and alighting on him," while a voice boomed from heaven: "This is my beloved Son, with whom I am well pleased."

Why did Jesus want to be baptized? The explanation he gave John was admittedly cryptic: "Thus it is fitting for us to fulfill all righteousness." Jesus, while faithful in observing Jewish laws and customs, was no conformist. He certainly displayed no interest in keeping up appearances and meeting other people's expectations. What did he have in mind on this occasion?

The *Catechism of the Catholic Church* offers this answer: "The baptism of Jesus is on his part the acceptance and inauguration of his mission as God's suffering Servant" (536). People naturally mark special occasions involving important commitments with ceremonies — for example, a wedding or an ordination rite. As participation in a ceremony like this indicates someone's transition from one state or condition to another, with particular duties and rights, so Jesus sought baptism by John as a way of declaring publicly that his quiet years of growth and formation in Nazareth were over.

Now, acting in loving conformity with his Father's will, he was inaugurating the public phase of his vocation as Messiah, the "Christ," the Anointed One of God. He was not the glorious, all-conquering Messiah of popular imagining, but a Messiah who "consents to this baptism of death for the remission of our sins" (CCC 536). This acceptance of his unique vocation was then sealed and confirmed by the Father's words, spoken from heaven for all to hear.

First Disciples

For some of those who came to John the Baptist, going out into the wilderness to hear him and be baptized was more than just a brief excursion in the country. They remained for some time, absorbing the Baptist's message and getting acquainted with others, forming a growing body of disciples. Jesus also stayed for several days after his baptism. And now, events made it clear that his own ministry had indeed begun.

One day, John was speaking with two of his followers when Jesus passed by. "Behold the Lamb of God," he told the others, pointing toward the stranger.

Taking the hint, the two young men left John and followed Jesus. "What do you seek?" he asked them.

"Rabbi, where are you staying?" Even this early, it seems, people had begun to recognize something special about Jesus and to address him spontaneously by the honorific title *rabbi*, "teacher."

"Come and see."

So they did, and spent the next several hours listening to him in growing amazement. We do not know what Jesus said on this occasion, but we do know the impact it made on one of his listeners. One of them, named Andrew, broke away to seek his brother Simon, like himself a fisherman from Galilee. Finding him, Andrew said eagerly, "We have found the Messiah."

Curious, Simon went to see for himself. For his trouble, he received an unusual welcome. "So you are Simon the son of John?" Jesus greeted him. "You shall be called Cephas." This was an Aramaic word meaning "rock" — in Greek, Peter.

Next day, preparing to leave, Jesus encountered still another young man, Philip. Like Andrew and Peter, Philip was also from Bethsaida, a town to the north on the shore of the Sea of Galilee.

"Follow me," Jesus told him.

Bursting to share the great news, Philip sought out his friend Nathanael and told him excitedly, "We have found him of whom Moses in the law and also the prophets wrote, Jesus of Nazareth."

But Nathanael was not so easily convinced. "Can anything good come out of Nazareth?"

"Come and see."

And Nathanael did. Seeing him approaching, Jesus said, "Behold, an Israelite indeed, in whom there is no guile."

"How do you know me?" Nathanael asked.

"When you were under the fig tree, I saw you."

We can only guess what Jesus meant. Perhaps, moved by John's preaching, Nathanael had been praying for light to know what to do with his life. Did this man Jesus have the answer? Was *he* the answer? Flabbergasted, Nathanael exclaimed, "Rabbi, you are the Son of God! You are the King of Israel!"

Perhaps Jesus smiled quietly at that: "Because I said to you, I saw you under the fig tree, do you believe? You shall see greater things than these. ... You will see heaven opened and the angels of God ascending and descending upon the Son of Man."

In the Gospels, Jesus repeatedly calls himself the "Son of Man." The title recalls a passage in the Old Testament Book of Daniel, describing a vision in which a Messiah-figure appears: "There came one like a son of man, and he came to the Ancient of Days and was presented before him. And to him was given dominion and glory and kingdom, that all peoples, nations, and languages should serve him." By referring to himself this way, Jesus was calling himself the Son of Man of whom the prophet spoke.

Now Jesus had begun gathering the men who would form the core group among his disciples. As he promised, they would indeed see remarkable things in the days ahead.

The Temptation of Jesus

But first, there was a direct challenge for Jesus. From the Jordan River, he was led by the Spirit into the wilderness, and there he prepared for the test by fasting and praying for forty days. Then Satan, putting aside his usual disguises, came forward boldly to tempt him.

In one of his homilies from his Anglican years, St. John Henry Newman not only called Christ's temptation a mystery, but declared it to be beyond explaining why temptation followed immediately after his baptism. Newman was right in saying that no single explanation exhausts the full meaning of this strange episode, but he was mistaken in suggesting that the most that is visible here is "a renewal, apparently, of Adam's temptation, in the person of the 'Second Man.'"

Recognizing that is recognizing very much, but there is more to be said about the temptation. If we accept the Incarnation (and it really *is* a great mystery that God chose to become man instead of redeeming us some other way), there is nothing surprising about Christ being tempted, nor even about the temptation's circumstances. After all, temptation comes with being human, and since Jesus was truly human, he could hardly *not* have been tempted. The Epistle to the Hebrews makes that point eloquently: "We have not a high priest who is unable to sympathize with our weaknesses, but one who in every respect has been tempted as we are, yet without sinning."

As for the timing of the temptation, there is a kind of internal logic in its coming immediately after the baptism by which Jesus publicly declared his commitment to his Father's will. Knowing, or at least strongly suspecting, that Jesus was the Messiah, Satan had his diabolical work cut out for him; but he was too clever a tempter to make the blunt proposal that Jesus simply abandon his vocation. Instead, Satan sought to induce him to pursue his vocation along different lines than those willed by his Father — that he be something other than the Suffering Servant of Isaiah's prophecy.

Satan began with a seemingly harmless suggestion that appealed to Jesus' natural desire for food after a long fast: "If you are the Son of God, command these stones to become loaves of bread." Here was a reasonable proposal to use his extraordinary powers to serve his own interests. Jesus replied by citing a passage from Scripture: "Man shall not live by bread alone, but by every word that proceeds from the mouth of God."

Next, Satan took him into the Holy City and, carrying him to the pinnacle of the Temple, took a turn at quoting Scripture himself — though he distorted its meaning: "If you are the Son of God, throw yourself down; for it is written, 'He will give his angels charge of you,' and 'On their hands they will bear you up, lest you strike your foot against a stone.'" Psalm 91, from which this comes, speaks of trusting God, not putting him to the test. Satan asked Jesus to be a wonder-worker — a Messiah who would win people to himself with awesome miracles. Jesus would perform many miracles, but to testify to his identity and reward belief, not to impress the impressionable as an itinerant magician might do. Now he responded to Satan's proposal with another Scripture quote: "You shall not tempt the Lord your God."

Exasperated, Satan next took Jesus to a high mountain and showed him a vision of the world's kingdoms spread before him in transitory, but real, splendor. Then, dropping the mask of subtlety, Satan revealed his true desire: "All these I will give you, if you will fall down and worship me." The truth was out; the Father of Lies himself had been obliged to speak it. *Worship me*. One can imagine Jesus' laughter before he gave the command: "Begone, Satan! for it is written, 'You shall worship the Lord your God and him only shall you serve.'"

Then, the Gospels say, angels came and ministered to Jesus. And Satan? Luke reports that following the temptation of Jesus, he "departed from him until an opportune time." We shall hear more from the tempter at other points in Jesus' ministry, especially during Jesus' passion and death. Here is a reminder of the warfare, usually concealed but sometimes visible as when Jesus cast out evil spirits, that ran all through the life of Christ and continues today. It is the titanic struggle between Good and Evil, which is destined to persist until the very end, when the Lord returns to pass final judgment. Already, however, its outcome is settled: "Jesus' victory over the tempter in the desert anticipates victory at the Passion, the supreme act of obedience of his filial love for the Father" (CCC 539).

Jesus' temptation holds a lesson for all of us, which Saint Paul expresses: "We are not contending against flesh and blood, but against the principalities, against the powers, against the world rulers of this present darkness, against the spiritual hosts of wickedness." These were the most determined, resourceful enemies to face Jesus as he set out on his mission to free humanity from sin and death; they are the same enemies facing each of us now.

Scripture

Matthew 3:1—4:11; 11:14
Mark 1:9–13
Luke 3:1–22; 4:1–13
John 1:19–51
Ephesians 6:12
Hebrews 4:15
Daniel 7:13–14
Malachi 4:5

4
Jesus Begins His Ministry

As he began his public ministry, Jesus was, says Luke, "about thirty years of age." The Gospels don't indicate just how long the public ministry lasted, but it appears to have been a little more than two years (at least) and little less than three (at most). Using clues in the Gospels, as well as contemporary sources such as the Jewish historian Josephus, it is reasonable to conclude that Jesus' ministry extended from early A.D. 28 until his crucifixion on Friday, April 7, in 30 (Supposing that the year, 30, is correct, we can be certain about April 7, since all four Gospels agree that Jesus was seized, tried, sentenced, and executed at the time of Passover, and we know when Passover was that year.)

Two or three years are not very many, but Jesus managed to crowd a lot into them, and the evangelists collectively record much of what he said and did. Even so, Saint John, still marveling at what he had witnessed, adds that if all the Lord's remarkable words and deeds were to be recorded, "the world itself could not contain the books that would be written."

After his baptism by John the Baptist and temptation by

Satan, Jesus returned briefly to Galilee and proclaimed the coming of God's kingdom, calling listeners to repent and believe. He also took steps to seek out the contacts he had made at John the Baptist's encampment, men he took to be promising material for disciples, and some of whom had apparently been waiting and hoping for such a summons.

Saint Mark, who later would be Saint Peter's companion in Rome and heard much of the story directly from him, gives a vivid picture of how the call typically took place: "And passing along by the Sea of Galilee, he saw Simon and Andrew the brother of Simon casting a net in the sea; for they were fishermen. And Jesus said to them, 'Follow me and I will make you become fishers of men.' And immediately they left their nets and followed him. And going on a little farther, he saw James the son of Zebedee and John his brother, who were in their boats mending the nets. And immediately he called them; and they left their father Zebedee in the boat with the hired servants, and followed him." Here and elsewhere, it appears that when Jesus called on someone to be his disciple, the response was usually immediate and wholehearted.

The Wedding at Cana

Soon after this, Jesus and several of his new disciples accompanied Mary, his mother, to a wedding in Cana, which was a town a few miles north of Nazareth. Weddings were social highlights of life in these isolated hamlets; celebrations often lasted several days. This required the groom to lay in a substantial supply of food and drink for the guests. But when Jesus and the others arrived, they found this particular wedding on the brink of disaster. As Mary quickly noticed, the wine was almost all gone. Disappointment for the guests and humiliation for the new husband threatened to spoil what ought to have been a joyous occasion.

"They have no wine," Mary quietly told Jesus.

But he replied, "O woman, what have you to do with me? My

hour has not yet come." That may sound like a brusque put-off, but the meaning was quite different. "Woman" was a form of respectful, even affectionate, address, while "What have you to do with me?" meant something like "What business is that of ours?" As for "My hour has not yet come," Jesus evidently wasn't planning to perform any miracles just yet.

Mary knew exactly what he meant. "Do whatever he tells you," she instructed the servants.

Six stone jars of water for use in purification rites stood nearby. "Fill the jars with water," Jesus told the servants, who promptly filled them to the brim. "Now draw some out and take it to the steward of the feast."

They did, and when the steward had tasted it, he confronted the bridegroom and said half reproachfully, "Every man serves the good wine first, ... but you have kept the good wine until now."

Since these jars held twenty or thirty gallons apiece, this miracle provided at least 120 gallons of excellent wine that the steward could now offer thirsty wedding guests. If there is a lesson here, it's that God does not do things by halves. No surprise that, as John recalls, after this miracle "his disciples believed in him."

In Jerusalem; Nicodemus

Passover was coming, and Jesus, being a devout Jew, went up to Jerusalem for the feast. ("Up" is literally correct, since the Sea of Galilee lies 690 feet below sea level while Jerusalem, set amid the Judean highlands, is 2,500 feet above.) In ordinary times — that is, between major festivals — the city's population was a hundred thousand at most. But at Passover, the greatest feast of the year, the number grew by many thousands. The pilgrims sought lodging wherever they could find it. Some camped in the hills outside the city, then converged on the Temple for the religious ceremonies. Coming to Jerusalem at Passover for Jesus was not only an act of piety, but an opportunity to teach and preach to sizable crowds from all over Palestine and abroad.

And by now, it seems, people really were taking note of this young rabbi from Galilee. Clearly, he wasn't part of the religious establishment centered on the Temple — priests, members of the minor clergy called Levites, and scribes. Nor had he studied Judaism's sacred texts under one of the recognized scholars. Yet his knowledge of Scripture seemed at least as broad and deep as theirs, while his manner in teaching was strikingly original. Unlike the scribes, forever citing the authority of the elders to support what they said, Jesus spoke of sacred things on his own authority; and his words, though sometimes mysterious, rang with truth. Soon enough, in the streets of the Holy City and in the precincts of the Temple, people began to ask: Who can this Jesus be?

One day a man named Nicodemus came to see him with that question on his mind. He was a person of some importance, being both a prominent Pharisee (more about them later), and a member of the Jewish council, the Sanhedrin, which handled matters of religious law and practice. Something about Jesus' words and manner had caught Nicodemus's attention. He wanted to know more; but John makes it a point to say that he came to see Jesus "by night," lest he be observed and criticized by other members of the establishment for hobnobbing with this outsider.

"Rabbi," Nicodemus began, "we know that you are a teacher come from God ..." and he went on to speak approvingly of the "signs" — miracles — that Jesus already was known to have performed.

Jesus cut him short. "Truly, truly, I say to you, unless one is born anew, he cannot see the kingdom of God."

This was how Jesus addressed someone in whom he saw potential. Never mind the usual niceties — go directly to the point. And the point Jesus now wanted to make (though Nicodemus was still very far from grasping it) was the need to be baptized in the Holy Spirit.

"How can a man be born when he is old?" the Pharisee objected. "Can he enter a second time into his mother's womb?"

Jesus was not about to be distracted. "Truly, truly, I say to you, unless one is born of water and the Spirit, he cannot enter the kingdom of God. That which is born of the flesh is flesh, and that which is born of the Spirit is spirit." And he went on to speak of this mysterious Spirit, likening him to a wind that blows wherever it will.

By now, Nicodemus was thoroughly perplexed. "How can this be?" he murmured.

But Jesus was not letting up. "Are you a teacher of Israel, and yet you do not understand this? Truly, truly, I say to you, we speak of what we know, and bear witness to what we have seen."

John's Gospel concludes the account of this incident with what may have been Jesus' parting words to his visitor or may be the evangelist's own commentary. It is one of the best-known and best-loved passages in all Scripture:

"For God so loved the world that he gave his only begotten Son, that whoever believes in him should not perish but have eternal life. For God sent the Son into the world, not to condemn the world, but that the world might be saved through him. Everyone who does evil hates the light, and does not come to the light, lest his deeds should be exposed. But he who does what is true comes to the light, that it may be clearly seen that his deeds have been wrought in God."

Walking home through the dark streets of Jerusalem with his head swimming from all he had heard, Nicodemus must have turned Jesus' words over and over in his heart. He probably asked himself — with a new urgency that surprised even him — Who is this man?

The Arrest of John the Baptist

When Passover ended, Jesus went into the Judean countryside

near the place where he had received John's baptism. Here he preached while his disciples baptized.

By this time, John had moved north to lower Galilee and the area called the Decapolis (or "ten cities"), where he continued to baptize and preach. One day, his disciples, apparently worried about a possible rival to their master, came to John with news about Jesus. John heard them out quietly, then said, "He must increase, but I must decrease."

Lately, John had added a new theme to his preaching: condemnation of the scandalous behavior of Herod Antipas, tetrarch of Galilee, and his illegitimate wife, Herodias.

Indeed, this situation was a public disgrace. Herod Antipas, son of one of Herod the Great's many wives, had divorced his first, lawful wife; Herodias had divorced her husband Philip, Herod's half-brother, who ruled the territory north of the Sea of Galilee. Now the two lustful sinners lived together as husband and wife, brazenly daring anyone to say they weren't. But John was not intimidated and denounced them openly and repeatedly. At last, Herod, encouraged by Herodias, had him arrested and thrown into prison.

The Samaritan Woman

As these things were happening, Jesus knew that, with the exception of a few like Nicodemus, hostility toward him was on the rise among the members of the religious establishment in Jerusalem. Foreseeing trouble if he stayed in Judea, he decided to return to Galilee. He had no illusions about how his mission would end, but for now there was still much to do — preaching the Kingdom, forming his disciples — before he gave up his life. Although John had been arrested, Galilee remained relatively safe, so back to Galilee he trekked, taking his disciples with him.

As travelers usually did, they took the direct route north through Samaria, though they were aware — who wasn't? — of the bad blood between Samaritans and Jews. For Jews, the Samaritans were apostates whose Jewish ancestors had intermarried with pagans and had mixed elements of Judaism and paganism, forming a syncretistic religion that Jews despised. The Samaritans returned the hostility, and clashes between the two groups had sometimes led to bloodshed. Now, with the Romans in charge, they coexisted uneasily, but tension was always near the surface. Although Jews could now travel through Samaria in safety, they neither expected nor received a friendly welcome there.

Jesus and his companions had paused at midday outside a Samaritan town called Sychar, near Mount Gerizim. Sending the others to buy food, Jesus waited at a field which, according to tradition, had been given by the patriarch Jacob to his son Joseph. The sun was high in the sky. It was noon. There was a well there, and Jesus, hot and thirsty after walking for hours, wanted something to drink. Just then, a Samaritan woman approached, carrying a jar for drawing water.

"Give me a drink," he said.

The woman looked at him in surprise. "How is it that you, a Jew, ask a drink of me, a woman of Samaria?"

That was a reasonable question. Jews avoided Samaritans, and men usually didn't speak to unfamiliar women in public. But Jesus was undeterred: For here was an opportunity for another of those conversations by which he led someone, step by step, up an inclined plane toward faith. What difference that the other party was a Samaritan woman?

"If you knew the gift of God," he told her, "and who it is that is saying to you, 'Give me a drink,' you would have asked him and he would have given you living water."

Puzzled, she said, "Sir, you have nothing to draw with, and the well is deep; where do you get that living water? Are you greater than our father Jacob, who gave us the well, and drank from it himself, and his sons, and his cattle?"

"Every one who drinks of this water will thirst again, but whoever drinks of the water that I shall give him will never thirst; the water that I shall give him will become in him a spring of water welling up to eternal life."

"Sir, give me this water, that I may not thirst, nor come here to draw."

"Go," he told her abruptly, "call your husband."

Lowering her eyes to avoid his gaze, she muttered, "I have no husband."

"You are right in saying, 'I have no husband'; for you have had five husbands, and he whom you now have is not your husband."

That touched a sore spot. Looking to change the subject, the woman decided to try religion, always good for provoking a Jew. "Sir, I perceive that you are a prophet. Our fathers worshiped on this mountain, and you say that in Jerusalem is the place where men ought to worship."

But Jesus would not be sidetracked into one of those endless quarrels between Jews and Samaritans; there were higher truths that neither side yet comprehended. "You worship what you do not know," he said. "We worship what we know, for salvation is from the Jews. But the hour is coming, and now is, when true worshipers will worship the Father in spirit and truth. God is spirit, and those who worship him must worship in spirit and truth."

Defensively, the woman replied, "I know that Messiah is coming; when he comes, he will show us all things."

The answer left no room for further argument: "I who speak to you am he."

Just then, the disciples returned with provisions. Seeing Jesus speaking with a woman, they were surprised, but they asked no questions. And the woman, leaving her water jar, hurried back to Sychar and told the startled townspeople what had happened. "Can this be the Christ?" she asked. And so, they went out to see.

Meanwhile, Jesus declined the disciples' offer of food. "My

food is to do the will of him who sent me," he explained. "Lift up your eyes, and see how the fields are already ripe for the harvest."

Then the townspeople arrived, and Jesus spoke to them. They had come from curiosity, but as he spoke, that changed. "We know that this is indeed the Savior of the world," they said.

He stayed in Sychar for two days, preaching and teaching. Then he and the disciples continued their journey to Galilee.

Jesus frequently said his mission was first to his fellow Jews, God's Chosen People. But this early episode in Samaria already indicates the universality of his message and the role that women would have in spreading it. This nameless Samaritan woman, with her water jar and a personal history of shame, has a permanent place in the story of Jesus as one of the first to bring news of this remarkable man to others.

Scripture

Matthew 14:3–5
Mark 1:16-20; 6:17–20
Luke 3:19–20, 23
John 3:1–29; 4:1–26

5

Ministry in Galilee

G. K. Chesterton once proposed a mind game to grasp how astonishing the early days of Jesus' ministry in Galilee must have seemed to people. Imagine, Chesterton says, that someone who has never heard of Christ sits down to read the Gospels with a mind open to the possibility that the events they describe really happened. For such a person, he remarks, reading the Gospel "would lead, if not immediately to belief, at least to a bewilderment of which there really is no solution except in belief."

Matthew's Gospel sums up Jesus' actions and the reaction to them like this: "He went about all Galilee, teaching in their synagogues and preaching the gospel of the Kingdom and healing every disease and every infirmity among the people. So his fame spread through all Syria, and they brought him all the sick, those afflicted with various diseases and pains, demoniacs, epileptics, and paralytics, and he healed them. And great crowds followed him from Galilee and the Decapolis and Jerusalem and Judea and from beyond the Jordan."

Plainly, the time was ripe for someone like Jesus to appear.

Messianic expectations were at a high point. The Jews expected a Messiah-King who would drive out the Romans and restore the kingdom of Israel, as it had existed at the time of David and Solomon. Only gradually did the Jews realize that this was not the kingdom Jesus had in mind, nor the kind of Messiah he intended to be.

Pope Benedict XVI calls Jesus' preaching of the Kingdom the "core content" of the Gospel and says it signifies God's presence and activity in human affairs in "a wholly new way" — a way best embodied in Jesus himself. This is a kingdom open to repentant sinners, to the poor, and to the lowly. The Second Vatican Council calls the Church "the seed and beginning of that kingdom" on earth (see *Lumen Gentium*, 5), while the *Catechism of the Catholic Church* makes the point that Christ "stands at the heart of this gathering of men into the family of God" (542).

Incident at Nazareth

At first, everything went well. People turned out in large numbers to hear Jesus preach and responded enthusiastically to his words. But when Jesus returned to his hometown, Nazareth, something ugly happened — something foreshadowing the betrayal that lay ahead.

It was the Sabbath. As usual, the men of Nazareth had gathered in the local synagogue. Jesus was there with them, so they invited him to read from the Scriptures. Taking the scroll, he read from the Prophet Isaiah: "The Spirit of the Lord is upon me, because he has anointed me to preach good news to the poor. He has sent me to proclaim release to the captives and recovering of sight to the blind, to set at liberty those who are oppressed, to proclaim the acceptable year of the Lord."

Having finished the reading, he resumed his place. Now, with the eyes of everyone on him, he said, "Today this Scripture has been fulfilled in your hearing."

Some of the listeners were impressed, but others muttered to one another, "Isn't this Joseph's son?" St. John Henry Newman says of their reaction: "They had lived so long with him, and yet did not know him, did not understand what he was. They saw nothing to mark a difference between him and them." Aware of their skepticism, Jesus commented, "Truly, I say to you, no prophet is acceptable in his own country," and he went on to cite examples from the Old Testament: the Prophet Elijah, sent by God during a famine to bring relief not to everyone but only to a widow in the city of Sidon; and the Prophet Elisha, Elijah's disciple and successor, who at a time when there were many lepers in Israel, cured only a Syrian named Namaan, commander of the Syrian king's army.

Outrage greeted Jesus' words. Not only was this man — the son of a modest Nazareth family whom they'd known for years — traveling around Galilee making lofty claims about himself, but here he was condescending to drop in for a visit home, and then insulting his former neighbors for not treating him as somebody special! Rising up angrily, they hustled Jesus out of the synagogue and out of the town, intending to push him off the brow of a hill. But "passing through the midst of them," Luke writes, he quietly went his way.

This incident at Nazareth is an important part of Jesus' story. Some who heard his message and witnessed his deeds welcomed him; but for others, it was as Romano Guardini says: "No matter what Jesus said — though he uttered words of divine power and profundity — invariably they were answered with stubbornness, distrust, and hate. No matter what he did — heal, help, pardon, shower with gifts — his thanks were hardness of heart, calumny, misinterpretation of his motives, blasphemy against the Spirit." Still, he was not about to give up. He continued to move among the towns and villages of Galilee, preaching the Kingdom and calling on people to repent while healing the sick, curing lepers, and expelling demons.

Capernaum, located at the northern end of the Sea of Galilee, was his base of operations. This town, with its buildings constructed of black basalt, offered easy access to other parts of Galilee, and was near a busy route used by travelers who could be expected to bring news about Jesus wherever they went. As for the "Sea," this was a somewhat pretentious title for what was, and still is, a modest body of water just thirteen miles long and seven-and-a-half miles across. Small though it was, it was home to a thriving fishing industry. Furthermore, it was a beautiful sight to behold, with its sparkling fresh waters ringed by low hills and its thirty-two miles of shoreline dotted by little fishing villages. Gusty squalls did sometimes sweep across those clear waters, raising waves and menacing careless fishermen who had delayed heading home in order to trawl their nets one more time.

In those days, Jesus worked many miracles of healing. Twice, he raised people from the dead: the little daughter of Jairus, an official of Capernaum's synagogue, and the son of a widow in the town of Nain, a village a few miles southeast of Nazareth. In this second case, Jesus was moved to act by the mother's tears. "Do not weep," he told her, then to her son: "Young man, I say to you arise." The young man rose, and Jesus gave him to his mother, while news of what he'd done spread from Galilee even to Judea.

The Call of Matthew

Jesus also continued to add to the small body of men he had chosen as disciples. In this, he applied his own standards, sometimes brushing aside conventional wisdom, as in the case of a tax collector named Matthew. Tax collectors were generally despised, for they not only acted as agents of the Romans in extorting people's money, but also made a killing for themselves by extorting a generous bonus for themselves. It's therefore easy to imagine the disapproval when Jesus, passing by the tax office one day, noticed Matthew and told him, "Follow me." And immediately, Matthew did.

But there was worse to come. To celebrate his new calling, Matthew gave a dinner for Jesus and his disciples to which he invited his old friends — tax collectors like himself, plus an assortment of other social outcasts. That was too much for the local Pharisees, who ostentatiously shunned such people. Confronting several of Jesus' followers, they demanded, "Why does your teacher eat with tax collectors and sinners?"

Hearing that, Jesus had his answer ready — an answer that was also a criticism of the Pharisees' practice of avoiding contact with people whom they judged unworthy. "Those who are well," Jesus told them, "have no need of a physician, but those who are sick. Go and learn what this means, 'I desire mercy, and not sacrifice.' For I came not to call the righteous, but sinners.'" As the Pharisees knew well, the words he quoted came from the book of the Prophet Hosea and were the words of God himself.

Exorcisms and Miracles

Jesus' exorcisms are in a special category, for here his ongoing warfare with the powers of darkness was strikingly visible. Theologian Germain Grisez calls these exorcisms a "frontal attack on Satan's kingdom." Clearly, the demons understood it that way, as was apparent in an incident at the synagogue of Capernaum early in the Lord's public ministry.

His hearers had listened intently as Jesus spoke to them, for, as Mark notes, "he taught them as one who had authority, and not as the scribes." The scribes were the learned expositors both of Scripture and of the compilation of Jewish religious laws and commentaries called the Torah; they were also the recognized authorities in religious matters. As Jesus spoke, a man possessed by an unclean spirit suddenly shouted, "What have you to do with us, Jesus of Nazareth? I know who you are, the Holy One of God."

Jesus rebuked him, "Be silent, and come out of him!" And,

with a loud cry, the unclean spirit left the man, convulsing him as it went.

The onlookers were dumbfounded. "What is this?" they asked one another. "A new teaching! With authority he commands even the unclean spirits, and they obey him." And so, his fame continued to spread.

Exorcisms were assaults on the evil kingdom of Satan; but what should we make of the miracles? Why did Jesus do these marvelous things?

One answer is compassion. Jesus did not look upon sufferers with the unloving, indifferent heart of a superior personage, above and apart from human misery, but as a fellow man whose heart swelled with feeling for others in their pain (as when he told the widow at Nain, "Do not weep," before restoring her dead son).

But he had another reason, expressed by Saint John's preferred word for the miracles: signs. These extraordinary acts pointed to Jesus' identity as God's chosen one, the Messiah. Yet there also was a certain danger here. People might come to think of him as only a remarkable wonderworker, whose sole purpose was to cure illnesses and pain.

In tempting Jesus to betray his vocation, Satan had asked him to accept that role and the cheap success that came with it. This was why Jesus often told people whom he had healed not to spread word of his healings — something that, moved presumably by gratitude, they often did anyway.

Curing a Paralytic

An early miracle, the curing of a paralytic, illustrates the different consequences that could accompany these acts of mercy. Jesus had been away from Capernaum for days. When he returned, a crowd eager to hear him speak gathered at the house where he was staying. Countless bystanders filled the doorway, making it impossible for others to enter. Then, suddenly, there was a scuffling noise overhead. Several of the thatched roof beams were set to one side, and, to everyone's astonishment, a paralyzed man on a pallet was lowered carefully to Jesus' feet. Several friends had brought him there, and unable to shoulder their way through the crowd, they decided upon this novel way of bringing the paralytic to the Lord's attention.

Touched, Jesus said to the man, "Child, your sins are forgiven."

Some scribes, men "learned in the Law," were present. Hearing those words of Jesus, their first unspoken reaction was disapproval: Jesus, they thought, was committing blasphemy, for he was claiming power to do something that only God could do — forgive sins.

Realizing what they were thinking, Jesus turned to them angrily. "Why do you question like this in your hearts?" he demanded. "Which is easier, to say to the paralytic, 'Your sins are forgiven,' or to say, 'Rise, take up your pallet and walk'? But that you may know that the Son of man has authority on earth to forgive sins" — he spoke now to the paralyzed man — "I say to you, rise, take up your pallet and go home."

And, Mark adds, "[the man] rose, and immediately took up the pallet and went out before them all, so that they were all amazed and glorified God, saying, 'We never saw anything like this.'"

Jesus had made his point. The paralyzed man and his friends rejoiced at the cure, while the rest of the people marveled at this sign that someone incomprehensibly special had come among them. But the scribes were left fuming, which would surely mean trouble.

Scripture

Matthew 4:23–25
Mark 2:1–12
Luke 4:15–30; 5:27–32; 7:11–17

Isaiah 61:1
Hosea 6:6

6

The Sermon on the Mount

What was the message that Jesus preached as he traveled through the towns and villages of Galilee, announcing the coming of God's kingdom? Unfortunately, there was no video back then, but still we know the central elements of his message from that magnificent compendium of his teaching — "a perfect standard of the Christian life," Saint Augustine called it — known as the Sermon on the Mount.

The Synoptic Gospels contain two versions of the sermon. Luke's, the shorter one, is said to be have been delivered in "a level place," while Matthew situates his longer version, occupying three full chapters in his Gospel, on a mountain. Mountain, plain — does it make a difference? In fact, it does. Luke's choice of a plain suggests the universality of the message, while Matthew places it on a mountain to emphasize a recurring theme of his Gospel: Jesus is a new Moses, delivering the message of the New Covenant from the side of a mountain, much as Moses brought the Ten Commandments of the Old Covenant down from a mountain.

Here we follow Matthew's version of the sermon as the longer, fuller exposition of Jesus' message.

The Beatitudes

Seeing the crowds, Matthew begins, "he went up on the mountain" and there began to teach. First come the Beatitudes, each beginning with the word "Blessed" (the state or condition signified by the word "beatitude"). Calling the Beatitudes "the theological and moral heart of God's kingdom," theologian Thomas Weinandy, OFM Cap, points to a "fundamental difference" between them and the Ten Commandments. The Beatitudes "enhance the significance" of the commandments; but more significantly, Father Weinandy says, the Mosaic law is perfectly fulfilled by Jesus' enactment of the Beatitudes "within his own life."

Here, then, are the Beatitudes:

> "Blessed are the poor in spirit, for theirs is the kingdom of heaven.
>
> "Blessed are those who mourn, for they shall be comforted.
>
> "Blessed are the meek, for they shall inherit the earth.
>
> "Blessed are those who hunger and thirst for righteousness, for they shall be satisfied.
>
> "Blessed are the merciful, for they shall obtain mercy.
>
> "Blessed are the pure of heart, for they shall see God.
>
> "Blessed are the peacemakers, for they shall be called sons of God.
>
> "Blessed are those who are persecuted for righteousness' sake, for theirs is the kingdom of heaven.
>
> "Blessed are you when men revile you and persecute you and utter all kinds of evil against you falsely on my account. Rejoice and be glad, for your reward is great in heaven, for so men persecuted the prophets who were before you."

Chesterton remarks bluntly that, with few exceptions, the doctrine of teachers of morality past and present amounts to a "solid and polished cataract of platitudes." But it's very different with Jesus. "If we could read the Gospel reports as things as new as newspaper reports," Chesterton adds, "they would puzzle us and perhaps terrify us," but they would certainly not appear as platitudes. Instead, they would be seen as paradoxical assertions turning worldly values upside down and asserting that the humble, disregarded people whom the world customarily treats with contempt (when it isn't simply ignoring them) are — or soon will be — the truly blessed ones.

The first Beatitude — "Blessed are the poor in spirit" — sums up the rest, so that St. Francis de Sales concentrates on it in his *Introduction to the Devout Life*. In contrast to those people, poor in spirit, whose blessedness Jesus affirms, Saint Francis says, "Cursed … are the rich in spirit, for the misery of hell is their portion." This is strong language for a saint justly famous for his kindliness and good humor. That in itself suggests the importance of the virtuous attitude — its traditional name is *detachment* — which this Beatitude commends.

Saint Francis has detachment in view when he says, "Whatever portion of them [worldly goods] you may possess, keep your heart free from the least affection toward them." Saint John Henry Newman makes a similar point in one of his homilies. Although, he says, the "goods of this life and the applause of men" are genuinely good things — as far as they go — there is no escaping the fact that they are always "short-lived." Then Newman sounds this cautionary note: "As the traveler set on serious business may be tempted to interrupt his trip to linger over a beautiful view, so this well-ordered and divinely governed world, with all its blessings of sense and knowledge, may lead us to neglect those interests which will endure when itself has passed away."

Principles for Daily Life

After laying his foundation, the Beatitudes, Jesus next applies their principles to various situations in everyday life. In doing this, he systematically expands and enriches the commandments of the Jewish Torah. "Do not think that I have come to abolish the law and the prophets," Christ says. "I have come not to abolish them but to fulfill them." Repeatedly, he calls attention to what he is doing — namely, filling out the ancient precepts by extending them with the formula, "You have heard that it was said. … But I say to you …" For instance: "You have heard that it was said to the men of old, 'You shall not kill; and whoever kills shall be liable to judgment.' But I say to you that every one who is angry with his brother shall be liable to judgment; whoever insults his brother shall be liable to the council [the Jewish Sanhedrin], and whoever says, 'You fool!' shall be liable to the hell of fire."

Other forms of misconduct are treated in the same stern fashion, which repeatedly passes beyond conventional moral standards. Thus:

- Adultery — "[Every] one who looks at a woman lustfully has already committed adultery with her in his heart."
- Divorce and remarriage — "Every one who divorces his wife, except on the ground of unchastity, makes her an adulteress; and whoever marries a divorced woman commits adultery."
- Casual oath-taking — "Let what you say be simply 'Yes' or 'No'; anything more than this comes from the Evil One."
- Revenge — "If any one strikes you on the right cheek, turn to him the other also."
- Love of enemies — "Love your enemies and pray for those who persecute you, so that you may be sons of

your Father who is in heaven."

- Almsgiving — "Do not let your left hand know what your right hand is doing, so that your alms may be in secret; and your Father who sees in secret will reward you."

The Our Father

Next, Jesus turns to that most perfect of prayers, the Our Father. Pope Benedict makes the powerful point that when praying this prayer, "we are praying to God with words given by God." Jesus introduces it by warning against making a show of prayerfulness ("go into your room and shut the door and pray") or multiplying words, as if saying more improved the chances of getting a favorable response. Instead, the Lord's Prayer is short and simple in its structure. The first three petitions speak of giving God the place of honor that is his due in the broader world and in our individual lives. The next four petitions present our needs and hopes and problems, asking God for fatherly help in dealing with them.

The prayer is this: "Our Father who art in heaven, hallowed be thy name. Thy kingdom come. Thy will be done on earth as it is in heaven. Give us this day our daily bread; and forgive us our trespasses as we forgive those who trespass against us; and lead us not into temptation, but deliver us from evil."

Next, the Sermon on the Mount offers practical advice on observing the genuine priorities of Christian living: "Do not lay up for yourselves treasures on earth, where moth and rust consume and where thieves break in and steal, but lay up for yourselves treasures in heaven, where neither moth nor rust consume and where thieves do not break in and steal. For where your treasure is, there will your heart be." Needless to say, this is not a condemnation of responsible saving to meet future needs. The point of the saying — as of much else in the sermon — is that we have to have our priorities in order: Save for the future first and foremost by leading a good life marked by love of God and love of neighbor.

This serves as an introduction to Jesus' famous words about trusting God. "Do not be anxious, saying, 'What shall we eat?' or 'What shall we drink?' or 'What shall we wear?' For the Gentiles seek all these things, and your heavenly Father knows that you need them all. But seek first his kingdom and his righteousness, and all these things shall be yours as well."

Similarly, in a passage mentioned earlier, the sermon delivers a blunt warning against judging others while excusing our own evil deeds. "Why do you see the speck that is in your brother's eye, but do not notice the log that is in your own eye?" This is followed by words of encouragement, expressed with a touch of irony: "If you then, who are evil, know how to give good gifts to your children, how much more will your Father who is in heaven give good things to those who ask him!"

Conclusion of the Sermon

Near the close of the sermon, Jesus offers terse guidance for obtaining a place in God's kingdom:

"Enter by the narrow gate; for the gate is wide and the way is easy, that leads to destruction, and those who enter by it are many. For the gate is narrow and the way is hard, that leads to life, and those who find it are few."

"Beware of false prophets, who come to you in sheep's clothing but inwardly are ravenous wolves."

"Not every one who says to me, 'Lord, Lord,' shall enter the kingdom of heaven, but he who does the will of my Father who is in heaven."

Finally, he warns against hearing him with the appearance of attention, then proceeding to do just as one likes; instead, his hearers (including us) must take his message to heart and organize their lives accordingly:

"Every one who hears these words of mine and does them will

be like a wise man who built his house upon the rock, and the rain fell, and the floods came, and the winds blew and beat upon that house, but it did not fall, because it had been founded on the rock. And every one who hears these words of mine and does not do them will be like a foolish man who built his house upon the sand, and the rain fell, and the floods came, and the winds blew and beat against that house, and it fell; and great was the fall of it."

When Jesus had finished, Matthew writes, "the crowds were astonished, for he taught them as one who had authority, and not as their scribes."

The Realism of the Sermon

Over the centuries, the Sermon on the Mount has had countless admirers, but it has also had critics. In modern times, the best known of these is the German philosopher and social critic Friedrich Nietzsche (1844–1900), whose strenuous advocacy of heroic moral nihilism Adolf Hitler claimed to admire. Nietzsche took violent exception to Jesus' moral teaching on the grounds that it expressed a "slave morality" that supposedly turned those foolish enough to accept it into wimps. "I do not like the 'New Testament,'" Nietzsche proudly announced, deploring the "almost voluntary degeneration and stunting of mankind" that he claimed was produced by the morality of Jesus Christ.

There have been many responses to Nietzsche's critique. Pope Benedict put his like this: "The true morality of Christianity is love. And love does admittedly run counter to self-seeking — it is an exodus out of oneself, and yet this is precisely the way in which man comes to himself. ... It is only on the way of love, whose paths are described in the Sermon on the Mount, that the richness of life and the greatness of man's calling are opened up."

Yes, someone might reply, but is this way of life realistic? In the Sermon on the Mount, Jesus tells us to "be perfect, as your heavenly Father is perfect." But how can any human being possibly do that? Good question! There are two answers.

First, as a recent writer on Matthew's Gospel, Leroy A. Huizenga, points out, the word for "perfect" used in the Gospel's Greek text comes from *telos*, which means end or purpose. Thus, Jesus is telling us to pursue our true end consistently and wholeheartedly — something we do by a lifestyle in conformity with God's law, which leads to eternal happiness in heaven, very much as God does by pursuing *his* end in creating us. "Perfection isn't meeting God's own standard of flawlessness," Huizenga explains, "but it does mean acting fundamentally in the way we should, doing as followers of Jesus' kingdom are supposed to do."

Second, Jesus does not tell us to be *identically* as perfect as God, in the exact manner of God; rather, he tells us to seek perfection in a fully human way that somehow mirrors God by sharing in God's mode of being and life. That is precisely what we do by living in God's grace — which, as the *Catechism of the Catholic Church* points out, is "a participation in the life of God" (1997). Jesus' call to perfection is something like telling a small child to be like his or her father or mother — not literally possible here and now, but increasingly possible as the child grows up. Similarly, the human lives of grace that we live here and now will be perfected by God in the kingdom of heaven. As the Second Vatican Council teaches: "When we have spread on earth the fruits of our nature and our enterprise — human dignity, brotherly communion, and freedom — according to the command of the Lord and in his Spirit, we will find them once again, illuminated and transfigured, when Christ presents to his Father an eternal and universal kingdom" (*Gaudium et Spes*, 39).

Jesus' way can be difficult. It is certainly challenging. But, with the help of grace, it is possible, and far more realistic than any alternative.

Scripture

Matthew 5—7
Luke 6:17–49

7

Apostles and Opponents

Throughout his brief but intense public ministry, Jesus had two great purposes in view. One was to proclaim the coming of God's kingdom and lead people into it. The other was to form a small group of chosen men who would continue his work after his death.

Traveling about Galilee, preaching in synagogues, healing the sick, and expelling demons, Jesus felt compassion for the people who came to hear and see him. "The harvest is plentiful, but the laborers are few," he told his followers. Now, he took steps to remedy that.

After a night spent in prayer, he summoned the disciples and chose twelve to be his apostles ("messengers") and pillars of the faith community that he would leave behind him. The number twelve recalls the twelve tribes of Israel. The twelve men chosen were Simon, now called Peter, and his brother Andrew; James, son of Zebedee, and his brother John; Philip; Bartholomew; Thomas; the former tax collector Matthew; Thaddaeus; James, son of Alpheus; Simon the Zealot; and Judas Iscariot.

After choosing the Twelve, he gave them their assignment: Proclaim the coming of the Kingdom to "the lost sheep of the house of Israel." He also gave them instructions on how to proceed: Take no pay for preaching, but depend on the generosity of those to whom you preach; expect hostility and rejection; trust entirely in God. And always have in mind his own mission, in which, from now on, they would share: "Do not think that I have come to bring peace on earth; I have not come to bring peace, but a sword" — not the sword of a military leader, as many who waited for the Messiah supposed, but the penetrating two-edged sword of God's word.

The Death of the Baptist

Scarcely had the Apostles begun their mission when two disciples of John the Baptist arrived. John, now in the prison of the tetrarch Herod Antipas, had sent them to Jesus with a question: "Are you he who is to come, or shall we look for another?"

Jesus answered promptly: "Go and tell John what you hear and see. The blind receive their sight and the lame walk, lepers are cleansed and the deaf hear, and the dead are raised up, and the poor have good news preached to them." Perhaps he paused there, and, smiling grimly, added, "Blessed is he who takes no offense at me."

Why did John send his disciples to Jesus? Some think that John, anticipating his own death, wished to shift his followers' faith from himself to Jesus. Others speculate that John, immobilized in prison and seeing his own ministry nearing its end, felt a need for reassurance that his life's work as herald of the Messiah had been fulfilled. Perhaps he had both motives. In any case, after John's people left, Jesus spoke of the Baptist with deep appreciation. "Among those born of women there has arisen no one greater than John the Baptist; yet he who is least in the kingdom of heaven is greater than he. … And if you are willing to accept it, he is Elijah who is to come."

That is, John was a prophet on the model of Elijah and was a man sent by God; and now, as people could see for themselves, here was the Messiah — Jesus himself. Yet many refused to believe, and, in refusing, they resembled the foolish people mocked in a children's song: "We piped to you, and you did not dance; we wailed and you did not mourn." Just so, Jesus declared, "John came neither eating nor drinking, and they say, 'He has a demon'; the Son of man came eating and drinking, and they say, 'Behold, a glutton and a drunkard, a friend of tax collectors and sinners!'" And now his disappointment mingled with righteous anger as he called out the towns of Galilee where he had preached so often, but to little avail: "Woe to you, Chorazin! Woe to you Bethsaida! And you, Capernaum, will you be exalted to heaven? It shall be more tolerable on the day of judgment for the land of Sodom than for you."

Shortly after these events, Herod Antipas had John the Baptist executed. The puppet ruler of Galilee had hosted a banquet, where the daughter of his illegitimate wife Herodias danced for the entertainment of Herod's guests, the leading men of Galilee. Hoping to impress them, Herod grandly promised to give the girl whatever gift she wanted. She consulted Herodias, John's bitter enemy, who told her to ask for the Baptist's head. And she did.

Herod hesitated. He had shown a surprising interest in John, even visiting him in prison to hear him speak. But, afraid of looking foolish to his guests if he reneged on his rash promise, he gave the terrible order. John the Baptist, the new Elijah, was no more.

By now, too, like storm clouds gathering over the Sea of Galilee, warning signs of danger had begun to converge on Jesus as well. The growing hostility of his enemies was apparent in a series of events on one Sabbath.

Some Pharisees had seen his disciples plucking heads of ripe grain in the fields and eating them. According to their reading of a passage in Exodus, this was a form of harvesting, and therefore not permitted on the Sabbath. They confronted Jesus: "Look, your disciples are doing what is not lawful." But he was not impressed. After citing examples to show that they misread Scripture, he further infuriated them by making an outrageous claim for himself: "The Son of man is lord of the sabbath."

As the Pharisees sputtered in indignation, Jesus entered the synagogue, and his adversaries followed, meaning to continue the argument. Inside, however, they encountered a man with a withered hand. Turning to the Pharisees, Jesus demanded, "Is it lawful to heal on the sabbath?" And before they could reply, he declared the answer: "It is lawful to do good on the sabbath." Then, turning to the afflicted man, he said, "Stretch out your hand." The man extended his withered hand, and suddenly it was strong and whole. The onlookers marveled, while the Pharisees, storming out of the synagogue, began arguing among themselves about how to be rid of Jesus.

Who Were Jesus' Enemies?

Jesus' enemies will play a large role in the rest of his story, so this is a good time to say something about them. We will start with the Pharisees, who appear repeatedly in the Gospels.

Not all Pharisees were enemies of Jesus. Many were good, decent people — indeed, among Israel's finest. Nicodemus, the honest inquirer who came to Jesus one night in Jerusalem, was a Pharisee. Other Pharisees passed word to Jesus that Herod Antipas was looking to kill him as he had killed John the Baptist. Nor should the Pharisees be blamed for requiring strict observance of Jewish doctrine and practice, or even for shunning contact with the Roman occupiers. Indeed, in the Judaism of those days, Pharisees were a force for reform and renewal, widely admired by the common people. Many (though not all) of the scribes, learned scholars of the Jewish law who are frequently mentioned in the

Gospels, were Pharisees.

But there were problems. Some Pharisees made a fetish of the minutiae of external observance, as if these things — at times, of the Pharisees' own invention — were the essence of religion. In some cases, too, this emphasis on externals had the unintended consequence of fostering pride and self-righteousness, as the Pharisees often courted admiration by flaunting their piety. Jesus' dismissal of religious formalism and externalism, together with his insistence that he had authority to do and teach as he did — authority that was his by right and not conferred by the expounders of the law in Jerusalem — was an affront to these self-righteous Pharisees. In time, they became Jesus' bitter antagonists, bent on eliminating him in order to preserve the true faith as they understood it.

Opposed in many ways to the Pharisees were the Sadducees, Jewish traditionalists who regarded only the Pentateuch (the first five books of the Old Testament) as fully authoritative. They rejected the oral tradition embraced by the Pharisees, denied the afterlife, and denied the existence of angels and spirits. Not all Jewish priests were Sadducees, but many of them were, and they were a dominant presence in the Temple. The Pharisees were popular among the common people. In contrast, the Sadducees numbered among their adherents many wealthy, well-connected members of the Jerusalem elite. And on the burning political issue of the day — what stance to take toward the Romans and the Roman occupation — the Pharisees avoided contact with the Romans, while the Sadducees stood for cooperation and accommodation.

The Gospels seldom speak of the Sadducees by name until near the end, when, as we shall see, they and Pharisees made common cause in seeking Jesus' death. If Sadducees and Pharisees agreed on little else, they were generally of one mind in regarding Jesus as a blasphemer and a threat to their interests. On both counts, he was someone they needed to eliminate.

The Battle Lines are Drawn

One day, people brought to Jesus a man who was mute, blind, and possessed by an evil spirit. Jesus cast out the evil spirit and healed the man, so that the man could speak and see. "Can this be the Son of David?" onlookers asked. Hearing that, the Pharisees sneered, "It is only by Beelzebul, the prince of demons, that this man casts out demons." Jesus replied calmly that he cast out demons by the Spirit of God, and for them to say otherwise was blasphemy. "Whoever says a word against the Son of man will be forgiven," he told them, "but whoever speaks against the Holy Spirit will not be forgiven, either in this age or in the age to come."

Jesus as agent of Beelzebul; Pharisees as blasphemers of the Holy Spirit — the battle lines were drawn.

If the Synoptic Gospels of Matthew, Mark, and Luke were our only sources of information about Jesus' public ministry, we would naturally suppose that, from his ministry's beginning up to the events of Holy Week, he stayed in Galilee without visiting Jerusalem. But John's Gospel tells us otherwise. According to Jewish law, Jewish men were to visit Jerusalem three times yearly for the so-called "pilgrimage feasts" — Passover, the Feast of Weeks, and the Feast of Tabernacles. Jesus, faithful to the traditions of his people, acted accordingly, using these visits to the Holy City as fresh opportunities to proclaim the Kingdom to pilgrims and the people of Jerusalem, while also engaging members of Jerusalem's religious establishment in discussion and debate.

John's account of events at the time of one Feast of Tabernacles demonstrates what typically happened on these occasions. During this eight-day festival in the harvest season, the small huts or tents — "tabernacles" — of pilgrims dotted the hillsides beyond the city walls, with the visitors coming to the Temple for religious ceremonies. As usual, Jesus busied himself preaching and teaching, which moved listeners to say, "Is not this the man whom they seek to kill? And here he is, speaking openly, and they say nothing to him! Can it be that the authorities really know that this man is the Christ?" Dismayed and angry at hearing that, the chief priests and Pharisees sent Temple guards to arrest Jesus, but he easily evaded them.

On the last day of the feast, a striking incident took place not far from the Temple on the Mount of Olives. Dragging before Jesus a woman who'd been caught in adultery, his enemies confronted Jesus, noisily pointing out that, according to Mosaic law, the woman should be stoned to death. So, what did he who claimed to forgive sins have to say? Bending down, Jesus silently wrote on the ground with his finger. But the accusers persisted. Rising then, he told them, "Let him who is without sin among you be the first to throw a stone at her." Again, he stooped and wrote with his finger. No one spoke. Then, one by one, with the oldest going first, the abashed men slunk away, leaving the woman standing before Jesus. Looking up, he said, "Has no one condemned you? Neither do I condemn you; go, and do not sin again."

When they were gone, Jesus and his companions walked the short distance from the Mount of Olives to the Temple. And here, still another clash with the authorities took place. Coming up to Jesus, several of them demanded, "Are we not right in saying that you are a Samaritan and have a demon?"

"I have not a demon," Jesus answered, "but I honor my Father, and you dishonor me. Truly, truly, I say to you, if any one keeps my word, he will never see death."

"Now we know that you have a demon," they cried. "Abraham died, as did the prophets. Are you greater than our father Abraham, who died? ... Who do you claim to be?"

His response rang out: "If I glorify myself, my glory is nothing; it is my Father who glorifies me, of whom you say that he is your God. If I said, I do not know him, I should be a liar like you; but I do know him and I keep his word. Your father Abraham rejoiced that he was to see my day; he saw it and was glad."

"You are not yet fifty years old, and have you seen Abraham?"

"Before Abraham was, I am."

"I am" — the name Yahweh gave himself in the Old Testament. Here was blasphemy on top of blasphemy! His outraged accusers seized stones to throw at Jesus, but turning away, he left the Temple.

A Man Born Blind

Outside, a man blind from birth sat begging at the side of the street. Most people ignored him, but occasionally a passer-by dropped a coin into his basket. Jesus stopped and regarded him with pity. Who is to blame for his blindness, the disciples asked — did he bring this on himself or was it his parents' fault? "It was not that this man sinned, or his parents," the Lord replied. Spitting on the ground to make paste, he anointed the man's eyes and told him, "Go, wash in the pool of Siloam" — a rocky reservoir in the southern district of the city.

The blind man did as Jesus said and returned seeing. When people who knew him realized what had happened, they rushed him to the Pharisees for questioning. As it happened, this day was a Sabbath, and the Pharisees, learning that the cure was Jesus' doing, predictably announced, "This man is not from God, for he does not keep the sabbath." Then they commanded the man born blind to say what he thought of Jesus.

"He is a prophet," the man answered.

Unwilling to believe a miracle had happened and hoping to find some other explanation, the Pharisees summoned the man's parents and asked them what they knew. But the elderly couple, fearing they would be expelled from the synagogue if they told the unwelcome truth, only said of their son, "He is of age, ask him." For a second time, then, the Pharisees hauled the formerly blind man before them and insisted he tell them what Jesus had done.

"I have told you already," the man said. "Why do you want to hear it again? Do you want to become his disciples?"

At that, the Pharisees began to shout abuse, but the man stood his ground. "Never since the world began has it been heard that any one opened the eyes of a man born blind," he insisted. "If this man were not from God, he could do nothing."

This was more than the Pharisees could bear. "You were born in utter sin, and would you teach us?" they demanded scornfully. Then they threw the man out.

Hearing what had happened, Jesus sought him out and asked, "Do you believe in the Son of man?"

"Who is he, sir, that I may believe in him?"

"It is he who speaks to you."

"Lord, I believe" — and falling to his knees, the man born blind worshiped him.

Deeply moved, Jesus told his companions, "For judgment I came into this world, that those who do not see may see, and that those who see may become blind."

But some Pharisees, observing the scene, took offense at that and asked angrily, "Are we also blind?"

"If you were blind," Jesus answered, "you would have no guilt; but now that you say, 'We see,' your guilt remains."

Scripture

Matthew 11:2–24; 12:1–32
Mark 6:14–34
Luke 6:1–16
John 8:31—9:41

8
PARABLES

In his great project of forming citizens of the Kingdom, Jesus used three principal tools: direct instruction (as in the Sermon on the Mount), healings and exorcisms (which gave visible testimony to his identity as Messiah and Lord), and parables. It's time to say something about the third of these — the parables of Jesus.

As the months drew on, people's response to instruction and miracles became dulled. Yes, crowds still turned out to hear and see Jesus. But even though some people took to heart what he said and did, many others heard the teaching and failed to respond to it. They observed the healings and exorcisms, but viewed them as little more than performances by an unusually gifted wonder-worker, rather than manifestations of God's power flowing in and through him. Clearly, something more was required.

And so, Jesus turned to parables.

In itself, this was not something new. Rabbis often seasoned their lessons with little tales, lively anecdotes, and colorful similes to illustrate their points and encourage hearers to apply the lessons to themselves. These were the *meshalim*, and Jesus was undoubtedly familiar with them. Indeed, says historian Henri Daniel-Rops, the parable-*mashal* was at that time so much a feature of rabbinical instruction as to be in danger of becoming "somewhat ossified and stylized," with the same figures and comparisons used and reused to the point of growing stale.

Jesus' parables were very different. As Daniel-Rops says: "There is nothing stereotyped or conventional about them: one feels that the comparison has sprung naturally from the mouth of the speaker; it is simple and exact, and the tone is one that cannot be copied." Reflecting life in the rural Palestine of the day, the parables often spoke vividly of simple, familiar things — shepherds and sheep, sowers and seed, good grain and weeds, fishermen hauling in a catch, country weddings, and the like. But for all the familiarity, the purpose was intensely serious: not to entertain, nor simply to tell edifying tales in the manner of Aesop's fables, but to require a decision on the part of listeners. Ultimately, that decision concerned the speaker and the new way of life that he exemplified and called upon others to adopt.

Let's take a look at a few of them.

The Sower and the Seed; The Great Banquet

The parable of the sower and the seed is a kind of keynote for Jesus' use of parables. It expresses his regret at the failure of so many to heed his message and be transformed, while at the same time challenging listeners to make a generous-hearted response. Together with the well-known parable likening God's kingdom to a mustard seed, and the parable of the wicked tenants in the vineyard (discussed below), it is one of only three parables found in all three Synoptic Gospels.

One day, a large crowd had gathered around Jesus at the Sea of Galilee. Getting into a boat, he put out a short distance from shore and from there taught the people. Mark reports his words like this:

"A sower went out to sow. And as he sowed, some seed fell

along the path, and the birds came and devoured it. Other seed fell on rocky ground, where it had not much soil, and immediately it sprang up, since it had no depth of soil; and when the sun rose it was scorched, and since it had no root it withered away. Other seed fell among thorns and the thorns grew up and choked it, and it yielded no grain. And other seed fell into good soil and brought forth grain, growing up and increasing and yielding thirtyfold and sixtyfold and a hundredfold."

"He who has ears to hear, let him hear," Jesus concluded, emphasizing the words so that there could be no misunderstanding.

Later, alone with the apostles, he explained his frustration at the obtuseness and hardness of heart that he so often encountered in his listeners. It was this, he said, that had led him to turn to parables, "so that they may indeed see but not perceive, hear but not understand." This was not a threat to abandon preaching, but Jesus' pained acknowledgment that even his ability to reach the people of his day — or any day, for that matter — was frequently exceeded by their unwillingness to be reached. The sower in the parable is Jesus himself, and the seed is his word. Then, as now, his word was often heard but not heeded; but also, in some who hear it, it truly takes root, grows, and bears fruit.

The parables fall into several distinct, though sometimes overlapping, categories. Some are parables of the Kingdom, likening it variously to a mustard seed, a buried treasure, a pearl of great price, a fisherman's net holding good fish and bad, or a field where weeds grow alongside grain. But perhaps the most striking image of the Kingdom, as recorded in Luke's Gospel, likens it to a great feast given by a wealthy man.

Invitations go out to a specially favored group of prospective guests (the parable's way of referring to the leaders of Israel), but the guests rudely decline, offering unpersuasive excuses. Angry now, the wealthy man sends servants to scour the countryside, with instructions to invite "the poor and maimed and blind and lame" (ordinary folk and Gentiles) to occupy the places intended for those who were originally invited. Pope Benedict sums up the enduring meaning of the parable: "The kingdom of God is at hand. A milestone is set up in the flow of time; something new takes place. And an answer to this is demanded of man: conversion and faith."

The Good Samaritan

Other parables focus on love of neighbor. Here, the parable of the Good Samaritan takes pride of place. To appreciate the challenge that this now-familiar story presented to its original Jewish audience, bear in mind the deep enmity between those worst of neighbors, the Jews and the Samaritans.

The circumstances in which Jesus told the parable are important. Luke's Gospel situates it in the Lord's fateful journey from Galilee to Jerusalem that was to end in his death. The route led through Samaria, where the people of one village turned a cold shoulder to Christ and the apostles, perhaps refusing them food and lodging and telling them, "Move on." Furious, the brothers James and John — "Sons of Thunder," Jesus called them good-naturedly — asked whether they should call down "fire from heaven" on the good-for-nothing wretches in that miserable village. Jesus said no; and a little later, replying to a rabbi's question, "Who is my neighbor?" he told the famous story.

A Jew traveling from Jerusalem to Jericho was ambushed by robbers — an all-too-common occurrence along that isolated and notoriously dangerous stretch of road — who "beat him, and departed, leaving him half dead. As they passed by, a priest and a Levite (a man of somewhat lower rank than the priest in the hierarchical ordering of Jewish clergy) saw the injured man lying at the side of the road, but each, averting his eyes from the sorry sight, left the victim and hurried on his way."

At this point, we may reasonably conclude that in failing to help someone so clearly in need of assistance, the priest and the Levite were grossly culpable; and indeed, so they were. But Jesus' point — one his hearers naturally would have understood — was rather different. In acting as they did, these two people weren't just displaying callous indifference to someone in bad straits; rather, they were moved by a deep-seated, religiously grounded fear of ritual defilement — a conspicuous instance of the spiritually crippling legalism that Jesus abhorred.

But now, a Samaritan came on the scene. Seeing the injured man, the Samaritan "had compassion" on him, bound up his wounds, helped him onto his donkey, and took him to an inn where he gave the innkeeper money and told him to care for the man until he returned.

"Which of these three," Jesus asked the rabbi, "proved neighbor to the man who fell among the robbers?"

There could be only one answer, and this man, learned in the law, gave it: "The one who showed mercy on him."

"Go and do likewise," Jesus told him.

The Prodigal Son

Another set of parables speaks directly of God's mercy. Here, the parable of the Prodigal Son is the best known, thanks partly to a famous painting by Rembrandt that depicts the climactic scene. And here, again, context is important to grasping the message.

Many sinners had been coming to Jesus, and he had welcomed them and extended forgiveness to them. To the scribes and Pharisees (now apparently shadowing Jesus to collect evidence against him), this was scandalous, and further proof that this upstart rabbi from Nazareth was no man of God. Knowing what they were thinking, Jesus responded through parables — about a man who loses one of his hundred sheep and rejoices when the lost sheep is found; about a woman who loses one of her ten silver coins and rejoices at recovering it; and finally, about a merciful father and his two sons.

In this third parable, the foolish younger son, now of age, had demanded his inheritance and gone off to a big city, where he squandered his money on high living and loose women. Finding himself penniless and deserted by the people who'd been his friends as long as he paid for their partying, he took the only job he could find — tending pigs, a terrible comedown for a Jew.

Coming to his senses at last, the young man headed home, rehearsing as he went what he would say to his father, "Father, I have sinned against heaven and before you; I am no longer worthy to be called your son; treat me as one of your hired servants." But his father saw him at a distance, and before the youth could recite his speech, the old man rushed to him, embraced him and kissed him. Then he told the servants to clothe him in the best robe in the house, place a ring on his finger and shoes on his feet, and slaughter a fine calf for a feast to celebrate his return.

As all this was taking place, the older son of the family was working in the fields. Hearing music and sounds of celebration coming from the house, and learning from a servant that this was all to mark his brother's return, he angrily confronted his father, "I've been a good son to you all these years, and you never did anything like this for me; but when this spoiled brat comes home in shame, you treat him like a king." To which, smiling gently, the father replied: "Son, you are always with me, and all that is mine is yours. It was fitting to make merry and be glad, for this your brother was dead, and is alive; he was lost, and is found."

As with Jesus' other parables, this one had an immediate application to persons and events at the time — in this case, the spiteful criticism of those holier-than-thou critics who condemned him for welcoming sinners and pardoning them. But it also holds lessons for all times and places. At different times in our lives, many of us have identified with all three figures in the story: as prodigal sons and daughters who wasted the gifts of their parents and their God; as angry siblings who resented the ready pardoning of a wayward brother or sister; and, perhaps, even as someone faced with the challenge of pardoning a child, a spouse, a friend, or a colleague for shabby behavior.

Thus, the parable is a call to conversion for everyone — those whose sins are notorious, those whose interior sins of envy and resentment gnaw at their hearts, and those challenged to show mercy rather than demand that others pay for their wrongdoing. As such, the story also is a timeless metaphor for the readiness of our Father in heaven to forgive us, his erring, repentant children.

The Wicked Tenants

Finally, in certain parables, Jesus reproaches the Jewish religious authorities for rejecting him. The harshest of these rebukes, delivered to the chief priests and Pharisees in Jerusalem shortly before his arrest, trial, and execution, is the parable of the wicked tenants.

A landowner plants a vineyard and leases it to tenants, then goes away to a distant country. At harvest time, he sends servants to collect his share of the crop, but instead the tenants "beat one, killed another, and stoned another." The landowner sends more servants, but they suffer the same fate. Finally, he sends his son. And seeing him, the tenants say among themselves, "This is the heir; come, let us kill him and have his inheritance." Then they murder the son too.

The symbolism here is painfully clear: the owner of the vineyard is God, the tenants are the Jewish authorities, the servants whom they treat so shamefully are the Old Testament prophets, and the son is Jesus himself. Having allowed that to sink in, Jesus faced his enemies and challenged them, "When the owner of the vineyard comes, what will he do to those tenants?"

"He will put those tenants to a miserable death," his listeners answered uneasily, "and lease the vineyard to other tenants who will give him the fruits in their seasons."

Grimly, Jesus drew the inescapable conclusion: "[The] kingdom of God will be taken away from you and given to a nation producing the fruits of it. And he who falls on this stone will be broken to pieces; but when it falls on anyone, it will crush him."

The others could not have known it, but the parable was a terrible foreshadowing of events that lay several decades in the future, in A.D. 70. At that time, Roman legions, bent on revenge for the ambush and massacre of comrades at the hands of Jewish Zealots, would lay siege to the Holy City. After inflicting a terrible scourge on the inhabitants, the Romans would conquer the city and level the magnificent Temple.

Then it would be as Jesus had said when he entered Jerusalem for the last time and wept over the city at the thought of what lay ahead. Using another figure of speech to express his feelings for Jerusalem and the great heritage of Jewish faith so often betrayed by those who ought to have joined him in its fulfillment, he said:

"O Jerusalem, Jerusalem, killing the prophets and stoning those who are sent to you! How often would I have gathered your children together as a hen gathers her brood under her wings, and you would not! Behold, your house is forsaken and desolate. For I tell you, you will not see me again, until you say, 'Blessed is he who comes in the name of the Lord.'"

Blaise Pascal, a seventeenth-century French religious thinker and author, says this in appreciation of the parables: "Jesus Christ said great things so simply that it seems as though he had not thought them great; and yet so clearly that we easily see what he thought of them." His parables, like his miracles, seek to touch the minds and hearts of those open to faith, transforming good dispositions into fervent acceptance of God's love present in him, while at the same time calling to repentance those who need to repent.

Scripture

Matthew 13:1–12; 21:33–46; 23:37–39
Mark 4:1–9; 12:1–12
Luke 13:18–19; 9:51–55; 10:25–37; 14:15–24; 15:11–32

9

Turning Points

As they had often done before, Jesus and the apostles had crossed the Sea of Galilee to the eastern shore, looking for a quiet place where they could pray together and get some rest. But that was not to be. People saw them go, and a noisy crowd was waiting on the far shore, eager to hear Jesus speak — and, if they were lucky, see him work a miracle or two. So, knowing the time left him was growing short, he took his stand on a hillside and, as always, spoke about the Kingdom and the need to repent.

Time passed; the sun had begun its descent. Pausing in his discourse, Jesus turned to Philip and, gesturing at the crowd, asked him, "How are we to buy bread, so that these people may eat?" ("This he said to test him," the evangelist John carefully explains, "for he himself knew what he would do.") Flustered, Philip pointed out that they didn't have nearly enough money to buy food for such a crowd. Then Andrew spoke up: "There is a lad here who has five barley loaves and two fish, but what are they among so many?"

"Make the people sit down," Jesus said quietly. There were five thousand of them, and they sat obediently on the grass. After offering thanks, Jesus told his companions to begin distributing the five loaves and two fish. No doubt they worried to themselves that the food wouldn't go nearly far enough, but by now they knew better than to correct the Master when he told them to do something. So, they set to work handing out the little they had, and as they did, something remarkable happened: Instead of running out, those few loaves and fish somehow became enough for everybody, with the leftovers filling twelve baskets. Awed by the miracle, the people prepared to hail Jesus as their king, but now he broke away from the crowd and went off alone into the neighboring hills.

By now, the sun was setting. Knowing Jesus would rejoin them when he was ready, the apostles got into the boat and headed for Capernaum. But the wind was against them, and they made little headway. Then — by now it was after midnight — they saw Jesus walking toward them on the waves. Peter called out, "Lord, if it is you, bid me come to you." "Come," Jesus told him. Clambering out of the boat, Peter took a few hesitant steps on the rough water; but as he became aware of what he was doing, his nerve failed him and he started to sink. "Lord, save me," he cried. Jesus rebuked him — "O you of little faith" — then grasped his hand and raised him. Together they climbed aboard the boat, the wind suddenly fell, and in an instant the boat's prow was scraping the shore.

The Promise of the Eucharist

When some of the people who had been with Jesus on the far shore reached Capernaum, they were surprised to find him already there before them. They crowded into the synagogue on the Sabbath, eager for an explanation.

Jesus knew they were curious, but by now he had something much more important in mind than satisfying their curiosity. "You were looking for me because you ate your fill of the loaves," he told the questioners. "Do not labor for the food which perishes, but for the food which endures to eternal life."

People began to beg him: "Lord, give us this bread always."

And there it was, just as he'd feared. He had performed signs — the multiplication of loaves and fishes being only the latest — in the hope of awakening minds and hearts to who he was and why he had come; but in the end, these people reduced everything to what was trivial and banal: *Keep giving us free food.* Hadn't he heard it before? "If you are the Son of God, command these stones to become loaves of bread."

Solemnly, therefore, he told them: "I am the bread of life; he who comes to me shall not hunger, and he who believes in me shall never thirst. I have come down from heaven, not to do my own will, but the will of him who sent me. This is the will of my Father, that every one who sees the Son and believes in him should have eternal life."

There was murmuring at that: Wasn't he just a carpenter's son? Who did he think he was, saying he came from heaven?

"Truly, truly," Jesus insisted, "I say to you, he who believes has eternal life. I am the bread of life. … I am the living bread which came down from heaven; if any one eats of this bread, he will live forever; and the bread which I shall give for the life of the world is my flesh."

This was really too much. "How can this man give us his flesh to eat?" they asked one another. But Jesus didn't attempt to soften his words, something he might easily have done simply by saying, "Don't worry — it's just a figure of speech." What he had said, however, was *not* a figure of speech but literal truth, soon to be accomplished in the Blessed Sacrament. Yet those first skeptics who heard his words that day and doubted do deserve our sympathy. Wouldn't we have doubted too? "Even if we had been prepared by teaching and miracle," Romano Guardini remarks, "we too should hardly know what to think."

Still, Jesus offered no compromises or excuses for disbelief. Instead, he doubled down on what he had said:

"Truly, truly I say to you, unless you eat the flesh of the Son of man and drink his blood, you have no life in you; he who eats my flesh and drinks my blood has eternal life, and I will raise him up at the last day. For my flesh is food indeed, and my blood is drink indeed. He who eats my flesh and drinks my blood abides in me, and I in him. As the living Father sent me, and I live because of the Father, so he who eats me will live because of me. This is the bread which came down from heaven, not such as the fathers ate and died; he who eats this bread will live for ever."

Several days passed while news of what Jesus had said in the synagogue spread and sank in. "After this," Saint John reports, "many of his disciples drew back and no longer walked with him." Finally, Jesus confronted the Twelve: "Will you also go away?"

There were many occasions when Peter said the wrong thing, but this was not one of them. "Lord, to whom shall we go?" he replied. "You have the words of eternal life; and we have believed, and have come to know, that you are the Holy One of God."

We may hope that Jesus took some comfort from those earnest, heartfelt words, spoken by the very imperfect man upon whom he meant to found his Church. Already weighing on him, though, was the terrible knowledge that even one of these men whom he had singled out to be his special companions was going to betray him. Considered in that light, his reply to Peter appears only too timely and to the point: "Did I not choose you, the Twelve, and one of you is a devil?" And lest there be any doubt, John adds, "He spoke of Judas, the son of Simon Iscariot."

Jesus' discourse on the Eucharist and the response that greeted it marked a turning point in his public ministry; from that time on, nothing was ever quite the same again. Nevertheless, he continued to preach in order to win new citizens for the Kingdom. He performed a second multiplication of loaves and fishes to feed a crowd of four thousand. He kept up his running dispute with the Pharisees, who, despite the many wonders that he had worked, still absurdly challenged him to produce a sign from heaven to testify to his authenticity. "An evil and adulterous generation seeks for a sign, but no sign shall be given to it except the sign of Jonah," Jesus replied, hinting at the three days during which his body was to lie in the tomb.

Peter's Confession

Meaning for the moment to put distance between himself and the people (among whom his fame had abruptly become notoriety), Jesus headed north, to the farthest reaches of Jewish Palestine. His destination was Caesarea Philippi, an ancient city about forty miles southwest of Damascus and not far from towering Mount Hermon. The city had been rebuilt by the provincial governor Philip and renamed to curry favor with the Roman emperor Tiberius Caesar. Here, Jesus decided to take a bold, potentially risky step: he would test the faith of the apostles — and in this way, he hoped, strengthen it.

One day, therefore, he said to them, "Who do men say that the Son of man is?"

Their answers reflected the current state of opinion: he was John the Baptist come back to life, he was Elijah, or Jeremiah, or some other prophet.

"But who do *you* say that I am?"

Again, it was Peter, the leader, who spoke up: "You are the Christ" — the Anointed One, the Messiah — "the Son of the living God."

Good for Peter! He had answered correctly, and his reward was quick in coming: "Blessed are you, Simon Bar-Jona! For flesh and blood has not revealed this to you, but my Father who is in heaven. And I tell you, you are Peter, and on this rock I will build my Church, and the gates of Hades shall not prevail against it. I will give you the keys of the kingdom of heaven, and whatever you loose on earth shall be loosed in heaven."

At last, Peter and the others understood that Jesus was the Messiah — and, as Pope Benedict remarks, "in a different sense from that of a mere bearer of some commission from God." How profoundly, radically different a sense this was would become clear only later, when they were witnesses to the miracle of his Resurrection.

For the present, though, he "strictly charged" the apostles to keep his identity as Messiah to themselves. For they still had a great deal to learn about what it would mean for Jesus — and also for them — that he was the Messiah. Only partly had their eyes been opened, for they continued to imagine a Messiah who would drive out the Romans and restore the Davidic kingdom in all its earthly glory — with part of its splendor being a royal court in which they would occupy places of honor. A Messiah who would resemble the mysterious Suffering Servant from the prophecies of Isaiah was still beyond their comprehension.

Jesus had much work to do with these men. And here, too, Peter's confession of faith was a turning point. From now on, Christ began to explain to the Twelve that he had to "go to Jerusalem and suffer many things from the elders and chief priests and scribes, and be killed, and on the third day be raised."

Hearing that, Peter was shocked and offended. "God forbid, Lord!" he protested. "This shall never happen to you."

No reward for Peter this time. Instead: "Get behind me, Satan! You are a hindrance to me; for you are not on the side of God, but of men." Satan indeed — for Peter's words were those of the Tempter himself, spoken now by the leader of the apostles. Jesus' response was new teaching: the doctrine of the cross.

"If any man would come after me, let him deny himself and take up his cross and follow me. For whoever would save his life will lose it, and whoever loses his life for my sake will find it. For what will it profit a man, if he gains the whole world and forfeits his life? Or what shall a man give in return for his life? For the Son of man is to come with his angels in the glory of his Father, and then he will repay every man for what he has done."

The Transfiguration

Several days now passed, during which Jesus let them ponder that teaching. Then, leaving Caesarea Philippi, he led them to Mount Hermon. There, taking with him only Peter, James, and John, he ascended partway up the slope of the steep mountain; and then the event we know as the Transfiguration took place. Luke tells what happened:

"About eight days after these sayings he took with him Peter and John and James, and went up on the mountain to pray. And as he was praying, the appearance of his countenance was altered, and his clothing became dazzling white. And behold, two men talked with him, Moses and Elijah, who appeared in glory and spoke of his exodus, which he was to accomplish at Jerusalem.

"Now Peter and those who were with him were heavy with sleep but kept awake, and they saw his glory and the two men who stood with him. And as the men were parting from him, Peter said to Jesus, 'Master, it is well that we are here; let us make three booths, one for you and one for Moses and one for Elijah' — not knowing what he said. As he said this, a cloud came and overshadowed them; and they were afraid as they entered the cloud. And a voice came out of the cloud, saying, 'This is my Son, my Chosen; listen to him!' And when the voice had spoken, Jesus was found alone."

As Luke is careful to note, the Transfiguration took place in the context of a prayer event, thus allowing us a glimpse into the heart of Jesus' own prayer. But more than that, this moment of prayer is special for what it tells us about Jesus — "the profound interpenetration of his being with God," Pope Benedict calls it — as well as about his unique mission as Messiah-Redeemer.

Moses and Elijah represent the law and the prophets of the

Old Covenant. They spoke with Jesus about his coming "exodus" in Jerusalem — the terrible ordeal that he would soon undergo to bring about our redemption from sin and death. Very likely, too, they foretold the Resurrection that would follow, that transcendent event sealing the New Covenant. The Resurrection was guaranteed here, in anticipation, by the voice of the Father, just as he had declared his approval of his Son's mission at the time of his baptism: "This is my Son, my Chosen; listen to him!"

It is often said that the Transfiguration was intended to reinforce the apostles' faith in Christ before the harrowing test of witnessing his terrible suffering and death. As far as it goes, that explanation is probably correct. But the Father's words from heaven — "Listen to him!" — also signal another, deeper meaning: an imperative to recognize him as a Messiah who redeems through suffering. "The Father is ultimately pleased," says Thomas Weinandy, "simply because Jesus is, devotedly and decidedly, committed to becoming Jesus — YHWH Saves. For this reason, the Father adamantly insists that Peter, James, and John 'listen to him.' Without the entirety of this knowledge, they will possess an inadequate, and even erroneous, understanding of Jesus and what it means for him to be, as Peter rightly professed, the Christ."

Very soon, however, Jesus entered back into the shabby reality of people's halfhearted faith. Descending from the mountain, he encountered a "great crowd" and, at its center, an agitated father from whose son the apostles had been straining without success to expel what they took to be an evil spirit. As Jesus approached, the man implored him, "Teacher, I beg you to look upon my son."

"O faithless and perverse generation," Jesus exclaimed, "how long am I to be with you and bear with you?" Then he had the boy brought forward and cured him. And as the onlookers marveled, he reminded the disciples of what was to come: "The Son of man is to be delivered into the hands of men."

And still they did not understand what that meant, and

were afraid to ask.

Scripture

Matthew 14:13–33; 16:13—17:23
Mark 6:30–52; 8:27—9:29
Luke 9:28–45
John 6:1–71

10

The Beginning of the End

"How long will you keep us in suspense? If you are the Christ, tell us plainly."

It was during Hanukkah, a winter festival also known as the Feast of the Dedication, and Jesus was making his last trip to Jerusalem before the Passover that would end with his death. While walking in the Portico of Solomon, a colonnade on the outer rim of the Temple enclave, he was confronted by priests and scribes seeking an argument. "If you are the Christ, tell us plainly," they demanded.

"I told you, and you do not believe," Jesus answered calmly. Then he reminded them of his miracles. These signs testified to his identity, he pointed out, so that those who believed in him had good reason to believe. Then he added a stronger truth about himself: "I and the Father are one."

Perceiving blasphemy, the questioners snatched up rocks to throw; but before any were thrown, he spoke again: "If I am not doing the works of my Father, then do not believe me; but if I do them, even though you do not believe me, believe the works, that you may know and understand that the Father is in me and I am in the Father."

At that, they sought to arrest him, but he slipped away. Time enough for that later, he may have thought. For now, putting the city behind him, he set out for the region at the Jordan River where John had baptized. For the next few weeks, he remained there, while many people came to him and believed in him.

The Raising of Lazarus

When would-be disciples declared that they wished to follow him, Jesus typically gave them fair warning: It wouldn't be an easy life, for the Son of man himself had nowhere to lay his head. But there was at least one house in Judea where he could count on a friendly welcome — the home of a man named Lazarus and his sisters Martha and Mary, located a short distance from Jerusalem in a village called Bethany. So now it was deeply troubling when word came from Martha and Mary that his friend Lazarus was seriously ill. Come at once, they begged him.

And yet, Jesus delayed. "Our friend Lazarus has fallen asleep," he told his companions. "Lord, if he has fallen asleep, he will recover," they reasonably replied. Then he said bluntly: "Lazarus is dead. But let us go to him." Fearing what might happen if Jesus placed himself once more within reach of those who wished to destroy him, the disciples hesitated and only reluctantly trailed behind him as he set out.

When they reached the familiar house in Bethany, Martha hurried out and told Jesus, "Lord, if you had been here, my brother would not have died."

"Your brother will rise again," he assured her.

"I know that he will rise again in the resurrection at the last day."

"I am the resurrection and the life; he who believes in me, though he die, yet shall he live." Then he told Martha to fetch her sister.

When Mary saw him, she fell weeping at his feet and repeated Martha's words: "Lord, if you had been here, my brother would not have died."

And now, Jesus wept too.

The tomb was nearby, a cave carved in a hillside. Mourners were gathered there, and Jesus told them, "Take away the stone."

Martha, always practical, pointed to the obvious: "Lord, by this time there will be an odor, for he has been dead four days." But at his word they nevertheless rolled back the stone from the tomb's entrance.

Raising his eyes to heaven, Jesus prayed. Then he called, "Lazarus, come out." And Lazarus, still wrapped in his burial cloths, emerged living from the tomb.

The Sanhedrin Deliberates

Learning of the miracle in Bethany, the high priests and leading Pharisees convened the Sanhedrin to consider their options in light of this new development. "If we let him go on like this," some said, "everyone will believe in him, and the Romans will come and destroy both our holy place and our nation." That was no idle worry, for if the Romans suspected the Jews were fomenting another uprising, they would undoubtedly respond harshly. Caiaphas, the high priest at the time, took charge.

"You know nothing at all," he told the others bluntly. "You do not understand that it is expedient for you that one man should die for the people, and that the whole nation should not perish." Neither he nor his listeners grasped the profound truth of those words, but murmurs of assent to Jesus' death greeted the high priest's intervention. Indeed, yes — let one man die for the many, and let that man be Jesus of Nazareth!

"So from that day on," Saint John writes, "they took counsel about how to put him to death," while also scheming how to rid themselves of Lazarus, whom this troublesome wonder-worker from Galilee had even — so the credulous mob insisted on believing — raised from the dead.

But why a death sentence? Why did Jesus' enemies want to kill him? Three reasons, not mutually exclusive, stand out.

The first reason was political. As suggested during the Sanhedrin colloquy that John reports, Jesus' increasing popularity among the common people made him a threat to the limited but real authority of the religious establishment. Ultimately, as Caiaphas pointed out, there was a real danger that the Romans, once sufficiently provoked, would get rid of them all and install a new, reliably Romanized power structure in their place.

A second reason, religious in nature, concerned Jesus' brazen disregard of the Jewish law as they interpreted it. His offenses included violating the Sabbath by healing the sick and crippled, ignoring rules of ritual purification, and consorting with sinners and Gentiles — even with the despised Samaritans, instead of shunning them in the manner of the righteous Pharisees.

And finally, a third reason, looming over everything else, was his perceived blasphemy, sometimes only implied, but often explicit. Ignoring recognized teachers who held forth in the Temple, expounding the law without reference to their interpretations, Jesus taught and acted like someone whose authority was his by right. And what right had he, madman or audacious pretender as he was, who not only called God his Father, but even made himself out to be divine? This blasphemy from Jesus, a self-taught nobody from nowhere, was intolerable, inexcusable, and clearly deserving of death.

Several weeks passed after the raising of Lazarus. By now, Jesus and his disciples had moved to a town north of Jerusalem called Ephraim. Soon it would be Passover, and there was speculation about whether he would risk returning to Jerusalem. Six days before the feast, he traveled again to Bethany for a dinner given in his honor by Lazarus, Martha, and Mary. During the meal, Mary anointed his feet with nard, a costly ointment whose fragrance filled the entire house.

Many of those present were moved. But not all. Frowning, Judas Iscariot grumbled, "Why was this ointment not sold for three hundred denarii and given to the poor?" He said this, Saint John explains, not because he truly cared about the poor, but because he was a thief who stole from the common purse. Jesus answered him sternly: "Let her alone, let her keep it for the day of my burial. The poor you always have with you, but you do not always have me."

Last Days in Jerusalem

Early the next day, Jesus set out for Jerusalem. A column of pilgrims was passing on their way there for the feast, and, recognizing the Lord, they saluted him enthusiastically. Seated on a young donkey, as the prophet Zechariah had foretold Israel's king would be, Jesus rode toward the city while those good people acclaimed him, waving palm branches and shouting, "Hosanna! Blessed is he who comes in the name of the Lord, the King of Israel!" But some Pharisees watched the spectacle angrily and muttered to one another, "Look, the world has gone after him."

As the impromptu procession neared the city walls, Jesus paused briefly to weep over Jerusalem — "Would that even today you knew the things that make for peace" — and warn of the terrible fate that would befall it in the years ahead. Then, going directly to the Temple, he further outraged his critics by driving out the money changers, busy converting foreign coins into local currency to be donated to the Temple, and the sellers of the small birds used as offerings in sacrifice. Although legitimate in themselves, these forms of commerce had expanded to the point of giving the sacred precincts the look and sounds of a bazaar. "It is written," he declared, quoting Isaiah, 'My house shall be a house of prayer'; but you have made it a den of robbers."

Later, he went to Bethany and spent the night at the home of Lazarus, Martha, and Mary. The next day, he returned to Jerusalem and, going to the Temple, he began to teach there.

But now his enemies confronted him: "Tell us by what authority you do these things." Jesus responded with that most grim of all his parables, the story of the wicked tenants, which we considered above. The priests and Pharisees knew perfectly well that the story was Jesus' warning to them that, just as their forefathers had repeatedly rejected and killed the prophets God sent them, so they, in their turn, were preparing to do the same to the Son of God himself.

Finally, then, the stakes in this struggle were out on the table and visible to all: Here was a conflict that could only end in death.

Now the Sadducees bestirred themselves. They could not tolerate the threat to their interests that Jesus represented any more easily than the Pharisees could. The Sadducees' first line of attack, reflecting their disbelief in an afterlife, took the form of an absurd tale about a woman and seven brothers who each marry her and die, with each in turn leaving it to the next in line to marry the woman and beget children with her, as the law required. When the Resurrection comes, the Sadducees asked, speaking of an event that they themselves thought would never happen, whose wife would this seven-times-married woman be?

Jesus had no use for such foolishness. There will be no marrying in heaven, he informed them brusquely, since all those who go there "are equal to angels and are sons of God, being sons of the resurrection."

And after that, Luke reports, the Sadducees "no longer dared to ask him any question."

As Jesus was leaving the Temple, one of his companions marveled at the awesome structure's size and grandeur. By now, however, Jesus was in a somber mood. "There will not be left here one stone upon another, that will not be thrown down," he answered.

Dismayed, the others kept silent until they reached the Mount of Olives, and there they asked him, "Teacher, when will this be, and what will be the sign when this is about to take place?"

The reply was a lengthy, disturbing discourse in which he spoke firstly of the terrible events during the first and second Jewish wars against Rome in A.D. 66–70 and 115–117, and then about his own Second Coming, when he would return in glory to pronounce judgment on the world. The discourse concluded with these awe-inspiring words:

"When the Son of man comes in his glory, and all the angels with him, then he will sit on his glorious throne. Before him will be gathered all the nations, and he will separate them one from another as a shepherd separates the sheep from the goats, and he will place the sheep at his right hand, but the goats at the left."

The exposition continues, with the King rewarding those who helped him when he was in need. When those generous ones, puzzled, ask when they did that, he will reply, "As you did it to one of the least of these my brethren, you did it to me." And those who refused him help when help was needed? "As you did it not to one of the least of these, you did it not to me."

"And they will go away into eternal punishment," Jesus concluded, "but the righteous into eternal life."

The Betrayer

While these things were happening, the priests and other Jewish men of influence were meeting in the palace of the high priest Caiaphas to plot Jesus' death. It was imperative to exercise caution in seizing him, all agreed, for otherwise, his followers might fight to save him. Just then, they had a welcome surprise: Judas the apostle had been waiting outside, and now, in the council chamber, he said, "What will you give me if I deliver him to you?" This was exactly what they needed — someone close to Jesus who would hand him over when and where that could be done safely.

So they paid Judas thirty pieces of silver and sent him on his way. From then on, he was looking for an opportunity to deliver Jesus to them.

What motivated Judas? Saint John says he was a thief who stole from the common purse, and his grumbling when Mary of Bethany used expensive nard to anoint Jesus' feet does suggest an unhealthy fondness for money. But thirty pieces of silver was the price of a slave, a paltry sum compared with the magnitude of his crime. Another suggestion is that Judas was furious at Jesus for his way of being Messiah — a way of nonviolence, forgiveness of enemies, and universal charity that clashed with Judas's preferences. This explanation looks more credible if we accept the idea that Judas had been, or perhaps still was, a Zealot, one of those fanatical Jewish militants expecting a Messiah who would drive out the Romans by force. It is easy to imagine resentment gnawing at such a man as Jesus diverged more and more from his notion of the Messiah.

But the best explanation may be that given by both Luke and John, which covers these and other possibilities: Satan had taken possession of Judas's heart and persuaded him to betray his Lord.

Scripture

Matthew 21:1–17, 33–46; 22:23–33; 24:1–51, 25:31–45; 26:14–16
Mark 11:1–11, 15–17; 12:1–12, 18–27; 13:1–37
Luke 19: 29–43; 20:9-19, 27–40; 21:5–33
John 10:22—12:19

11

Last Supper, Trial, and Crucifixion

The week moved swiftly to its shattering climax. At midweek, Jesus and the Twelve gathered for their evening meal in the large Upper Room, part of a house said to belong to the family of Mark the evangelist. Scholars differ on which day of the week it was, and on whether the meal was or wasn't, strictly speaking, a Passover meal. Whatever the case, Jesus clearly intended it as a solemn occasion with his closest friends, intimately linked to his redemptive Sacrifice — his own Passover, as it were.

Even before the meal began, something extraordinary happened. Tying a towel around his waist and carrying a basin of water, Jesus knelt before each apostle in turn and washed his feet. Peter objected to this gesture of humility by the man whom he called Master, but Jesus insisted. For there was an important lesson in what he did. "You call me Teacher and Lord," he told the startled group, "and you are right, for so I am. If I then, your Lord and Teacher, have washed your feet, you also ought to wash one another's feet."

Then, having joined the others at the table, Jesus made a shocking announcement: "Truly, truly, I say to you, one of you will betray me." Peter signaled to John, who was next to Jesus, to ask who it was, and John did. Saying it was the one to whom he would give a morsel of bread, Jesus dipped a morsel in the bowl of sauce they shared and handed it to Judas. Frowning, Judas muttered some excuse and hurried out of the room. Unaware of what had just happened, the rest supposed Jesus had sent him on an errand — to give alms to the poor, perhaps. Peter, shocked but never at a loss for words, offered his assurances to Jesus: "I will lay down my life for you." Looking at him sadly, Jesus replied, "The cock will not crow till you have denied me three times."

Conversation was subdued after that, for by now the apostles understood that this was no ordinary meal. As it drew to a close, Jesus took unleavened bread, blessed it, and broke it, then distributed it to them, saying, "Take, eat; this is my body." Next, he raised a cup of wine, blessed it, and gave it to them with the words: "Drink of it, all of you; for this is my blood of the covenant, which is poured out for many for the forgiveness of sins."

After this, Jesus began his Last Supper discourse.

He spoke of many things: consolation for the apostles ("Peace I leave with you; my peace I give to you"); his new commandment of love ("Love one another as I have loved you," coupled with a reminder that no love is greater than the love that moves someone to lay down his life for friends); a prediction that "the world" would hate and persecute them as it hated and persecuted him; the promise of the Holy Spirit; and an exhortation to unity. Addressing his Father on behalf of those he now called friends, he said: "I do not pray that you should take them out of the world, but that you should keep them from the evil one. They are not of the world, even as I am not of the world. Sanctify them in the truth; your word is truth. As you sent me into the world, so I have sent them into the world. And for their sake I consecrate myself, that they also may be consecrated in truth."

When the discourse ended, Jesus and the apostles left the Upper Room and, crossing the Kidron valley, went to a garden called Gethsemane, a secluded spot on the Mount of Olives where they had often gathered. Taking Peter, James, and John with him, Jesus went apart and prayed: "My Father, if it be possible, let this chalice pass from me; nevertheless, not as I will, but as you will." Returning to the three apostles, he found them sleeping. "Rise," he told them, "and pray that you may not enter into temptation."

Suddenly, there was a disturbance at the garden's entrance. Bearing torches and armed with swords and clubs, a motley crowd — Temple guards, priests, Pharisees, Sadducees — burst into the garden, bent on seizing Jesus. Drawing his sword, Peter slashed at one of them, cutting off his ear. "No more of this!" Jesus commanded, and reaching out, he touched the injured man and healed him. Then, to the crowd: "This is your hour, and the power of darkness." The crowd bound him and dragged him away while the terrified apostles fled into the night.

The Trial

First, Jesus' captors took him to Annas, Caiaphas's father-in-law. Annas had been high priest himself until the Romans deposed him, and he remained an influential figure in Jerusalem, deeply involved in the plot to kill Jesus. After a preliminary interrogation of the prisoner, he sent Jesus on to the palace of the high priest, where as many members of the Sanhedrin as could be assembled on short notice were waiting.

The trial that followed was a shabby affair, featuring false witnesses who contradicted one another and focused on Jesus' alleged blasphemy. "This fellow said, 'I am able to destroy the temple of God, and to build it in three days,'" two witnesses testified. And yes — Jesus really had said something like that, but referring to his own death and resurrection. Still, it was enough for Caiaphas. "Are you the Christ, the Son of the Blessed?" he shouted. Looking at him steadily, Jesus replied, "I am; and you will see the Son of man sitting at the right hand of Power, and coming with the clouds of heaven." Then the high priest tore his vestments, a formal gesture signifying horror, while crying out in triumph: "Why do we still need witnesses? You have heard the blasphemy. What is your decision?"

But that was never in doubt: the sentence was death. And now, some of the judges spat on Jesus and struck him.

When Jesus was seized, Peter had fled along with the others; but, careful not to be seen, he trailed captors and captive to Annas's house and then to the high priest's palace. To his credit, he was determined not to abandon Christ, but he had no idea what, if anything, he could do to help. Step forward as a character witness? That would be useless, and was much too risky besides. So, as the sham trial proceeded, he stood nervously in the courtyard of the palace, warming himself at a charcoal fire along with a few servants and Temple guards.

Three times, a servant girl confronted Peter and accused him of being a follower of Jesus — his accent itself gave him away as a Galilean — and three times, Peter denied it. "I do not know the man," he insisted. After the third denial, a cock crowed; and through a door that opened on the room where the trial was taking place, Jesus' gaze met his. Now Peter remembered the Lord's warning — "Three times you will deny me" — and going out, he wept bitterly.

By the terms of the Roman occupation, the Jewish authorities had no authority to execute anyone — the Romans reserved that to themselves. So Jesus' accusers next hustled him to the Antonia fortress, a massive building at one corner of the Temple grounds. The Antonia housed the local garrison of Roman soldiers, and was also the residence of the Roman prefect when he was in Jerusalem — somewhere the prefect made it a point to be at Passover, in case religious fervor during this feast, so fraught with national significance for Jews, turned into an uprising requiring forceful suppression. The current prefect, Pontius Pilate, was no friend of the Jews and had a record of cruelty (so much so that a few years later the emperor would banish him to Gaul, where he is said to have killed himself). Just now, however, he wished to avoid trouble lest yet another ugly incident further damage his reputation with his superiors in Rome.

By now, it was early morning. The Jews, unwilling to enter the praetorium for fear of suffering defilement that would prevent them from eating the Passover meal that night, waited outside the Antonia with their prisoner. Besides members of the Sanhedrin, the crowd included guards, minor clergy, and other functionaries and hangers-on who could be trusted to do as Caiaphas and the other leaders wanted.

The accusers knew charging Jesus with blasphemy wouldn't get them what they wanted: his death. Blasphemy was a religious offense, and thus of no concern to the Romans. It was necessary that Pilate be persuaded that the prisoner was a potential insurrectionist and a threat to Rome. Pilate took his time about coming out, but finally he appeared, so they started in: "We found this man perverting our nation, and forbidding us to give tribute to Caesar, and saying that he himself is Christ a king."

Pilate listened, but he wasn't convinced. Going back inside, he had Jesus brought to him. "Are you the King of the Jews?" he asked.

"My kingship is not of this world," Jesus answered. "If my kingdom were of this world, my servants would fight, that I not be handed over to the Jews; but my kingship is not from the world."

"So you are a king?"

"You say that I am a king. For this I was born, and for this I have come into the world, to bear witness to the truth."

Pilate shrugged: "What is truth?" But at least, by now, he saw the truth of this situation: Jesus was no insurrectionist, and the complaints of the high priest and his crowd arose from some obscure religious squabble among these troublesome Jews. At this point, too, Pilate's wife took him aside to tell him of a warning she had received in a dream. "Have nothing to do with that righteous man," she urged him.

Now Pilate had an idea. Jesus was a Galilean, and Herod Antipas, the provincial governor of Galilee, was in the city for Passover. And so Pilate sent Jesus to Herod, hoping the puppet ruler would know what to do with him. Herod was pleased, since he had heard much about Jesus and was hoping to see him work one of his famous miracles. But Jesus said nothing, while his accusers stood by heaping charges on him. So, clothing him in a gaudy robe, Herod had him mocked and beaten, then sent him back to Pilate. Relations between the two men had been strained up to now, but, as Saint Luke notes, they were friends from that day on.

Next, Pilate saw another possibility. It was customary for him to pardon a prisoner at Passover. Among the prisoners then in the Antonia's cells was one Barabbas, an authentic insurrectionist (and a murderer to boot). Confronting the crowd again, Pilate offered a choice: Jesus or Barabbas? "Release to us Barabbas" was the response. Frustrated, Pilate next had Jesus scourged. This punishment was executed with a whip whose ends were flesh-tearing scraps of bone and metal. It was not uncommon for prisoners to die from scourging alone. After the scourging, the soldiers clothed Jesus in a purple robe, jammed a crown of thorns onto his head, and took turns pummeling him while shouting, "Hail, King of the Jews."

When the soldiers grew tired of this sport, Pilate took him outside and showed him to the crowd. "I find no crime in him," he declared, adding, "Here is the man." Still, the agitated crowd only shouted, "Crucify him, crucify him!" As the prefect hesitated, someone called out a threat: "If you release this man, you are not Caesar's friend." That touched Pilate where he was most vulnerable. "Shall I crucify your King?" the Roman sneered. And the chief priests replied, "We have no king but Caesar."

Pilate was buckling. Plainly, Jesus had done nothing deserving of death, but the Jews were turning ugly, and he sensed that he was losing control of the situation. What did one Jew matter? So he told the soldiers to take the man away and crucify him. Then, with the crowd watching, he ostentatiously washed his hands in a basin of water. But before the sorry procession set off for the place of execution, he wrote an inscription to be hung around the condemned man's neck: "Jesus of Nazareth, the King of the Jews." The Jews grumbled at that, but Pilate, anxious to salvage what pride he had left, insisted, so the inscription stayed. Neither he nor the crowd knew it, but the inscription spoke the simple truth.

Meanwhile, a very different drama was being enacted in another part of the Temple enclave. Caiaphas, Annas, and the rest had retired there to review the events of the day and congratulate themselves on getting rid of Jesus. Suddenly, Judas burst in. "I have sinned in betraying innocent blood," he cried. "What is that to us?" they answered. Flinging down the thirty pieces of silver, Judas went away and hanged himself. Learning later what he had done, the priests, ever scrupulous about observing the law, agreed it would be wrong to put blood money into the Temple treasury. So they used the silver pieces to buy a potter's field for burying strangers who died while visiting Jerusalem.

The Crucifixion

Jesus, weak from the scourging and staggering under the weight of the cross beam from which he soon would hang, made his way haltingly to the execution site. Several times he fell, so the soldiers laid hands on one Simon, a visitor from Cyrene (a coastal city in what is now Libya) who had paused to watch the spectacle, and forced him to carry the heavy beam the rest of the way. Saint Mark notes without further explanation that this Simon was the father of Alexander and Rufus — apparently two men well known to the community of Jewish Christians in Rome for whom he wrote.

The procession made its way to a hill outside the city walls called Golgotha, "skull" in Aramaic, *Calvariae*, or Calvary, in Latin. There the soldiers nailed Jesus to the cross beam and hung Pilate's inscription above his head. Then, having divided his clothes among themselves — except for the tunic, woven without seam, for which they cast lots — they hoisted the beam bearing Jesus into position.

Crucifixion was an agonizing way to die. The Roman empire used this very public mode of execution to dispatch insurrectionists and discourage others who might think of rebelling. Death came slowly and painfully from asphyxiation and loss of blood. Although the condemned individual typically received wine mixed with a narcotic to lessen the pain, Jesus (evidently determined to suffer this hideous experience to the full) refused it.

Two robbers were crucified along with him, one on either side. Matthew and Mark note that, at first, both robbers "reviled him." Eventually, however, one of them (known in tradition as Dismas) felt his heart soften toward Jesus. As the one thief shouted, "Are you not the Christ? Save yourself and us," Dismas rebuked him. We're getting what we deserve, he said, but "this man has done nothing wrong." Then he addressed the Lord: "Jesus, remember me when you come in your kingly power." And this small expression of faith and compassion received an extraordinary response: "Truly, I say to you, today you will be with me in Paradise."

Some from the Temple were there, and they passed the time mocking Jesus. "He saved others; he cannot save himself. He is the King of Israel; let him come down now from the cross, and we will believe in him. He trusts in God; let God deliver him now." Newman calls Jesus' "atoning sacrifice" the "vital principle on which the Christian lives, and without which Christianity is not." So it comes as no surprise that the Tempter's voice was audible in these taunts, once again proposing that Christ save himself by compromising his messianic mission — to win the world's redemption by loving fidelity to the Father's will, no matter the cost to himself.

A handful of sympathetic onlookers kept watch with Jesus. Saint John speaks of "his mother, and his mother's sister, Mary the wife of Clopas, and Mary Magdalene"; also part of the group was the Beloved Disciple, Saint John himself. And even in his agony, Jesus managed to think of others. For his tormenters, he prayed, "Father, forgive them, for they know not what they do." And as the end drew near, he addressed his mother: "Woman, behold your son!" and to John: "Behold, your mother!" From that day, John writes, "the disciple took her to his own home."

By Mark's count, Jesus had been on the cross nearly six hours by now. His face and body were bloody and lacerated, his thirst was excruciating, his chest heaved as he struggled to breathe, and only with difficulty could he speak. "I thirst," he gasped. A soldier raised a spear bearing hyssop soaked in sour wine to his lips. Then Jesus called out in Aramaic, "*Eloi, Eloi, lama sabachthani?*" — "My God, my God, why have you forsaken me?" And murmuring, "It is finished," he bowed his head and gave up his spirit.

That final cry from the cross was not a cry of despair. The sense of God's absence, the Father's silence as Jesus hung on the cross — there was now no "This is my Son in whom I am well pleased" — was part of his torment as well as the ultimate test of his loving obedience; Thomas Weinandy calls it "Jesus' final temptation." But the words that he cried out from the cross are the opening words of Psalm 22, a messianic psalm that speaks of the Messiah's suffering, but concludes with a soaring affirmation of faith and trust in the Father:

Yet you are holy,

enthroned on the praises of Israel.
In you our fathers trusted;
they trusted and thou didst deliver them.
To you they cried and were saved;
in you they trusted, and were not disappointed. …
For he has not despised or abhorred
the affliction of the afflicted;
and he has not hidden his face from him,
but has heard, when he cried to him.

By his human act of embracing the Father's will, Jesus accomplished our redemption. "Truly this man was the Son of God!" exclaimed the centurion who commanded the squad of soldiers on Calvary. It was the voice of one of the guilty ones speaking for us all.

Since this was the day of Preparation for the Passover and the impending Sabbath was a major feast, the Jews were anxious that the bodies of the dead not be left hanging on their crosses, so Pilate ordered that the legs of the three crucified men be broken to hasten death. The soldiers broke the robbers' legs, but coming to Jesus, they found he had already died. Still, to be sure, one of them pierced his side with a spear, and blood and water flowed out.

Now two members of the Sanhedrin arrived who hadn't been part of the plot against Jesus — a wealthy man named Joseph of Arimathea, who offered a new tomb not far away, and Nicodemus, who had once come to Jesus at night, but now, no longer afraid of being seen, brought myrrh and aloes for the burial. So the little group took Jesus' body to the tomb, wrapped his body in linen cloths together with the spices, and rolled a stone in front of the tomb's entrance. Then they left in silence and sorrow.

Scripture

Matthew 26:20—27:61
Mark 14:17–47
Luke 22:14–23, 56
John 13:1—17:26; 18:12—19:42
Psalm 22: 3–5, 24

12

The Resurrection and Ascension

N. T. Wright, New Testament scholar and Anglican bishop, calls the resurrection of Jesus Christ "the turning point of world history." With good reason; for, as Pope St. John Paul II says in his encyclical on God's mercy, *Dives in Misericordia*, Christ, "who in his Passion and the torment of the Cross did not obtain human mercy, has revealed in his Resurrection the fullness of the love that the Father has for him and, in him, for all people."

In what they tell us about the Resurrection and post-Resurrection events, the four Gospels differ greatly from one another and from the account in Saint Paul's first letter to the Corinthians. But the cumulative effect of these sources is to reinforce the central fact of the story that they all tell; for if first-century Christians had wished to spread a fiction about Christ rising from the dead, they would have been careful to eliminate the differences. As it is, the Gospels are compelling testimony to one fundamental fact: Jesus Christ rose from the dead.

Considered in themselves, the differences are no surprise. Anyone who has had the experience of collecting evidence of the same event from several eyewitnesses knows how different each witness's account can be from the rest. It is important, too, to realize that the period from Jesus' rising from the tomb to his ascension to heaven was not a continuation of his previous life, when it was generally known where he was and what he was doing, but a time when Jesus, alive now in a new and different way, appeared at intervals to others according to a plan known only to himself. As Romano Guardini says, Jesus was "first in one place, then in another; making mysterious transitions from some otherwhere into the here, and then disappearing again."

But the central elements surrounding the Resurrection itself are the same in all the Gospels. The narrative begins at the tomb very early Sunday morning, the day after the Jewish Sabbath. Mary Magdalene and several other women had come to finish preparing Jesus' body for burial. Entering the garden, they worried about how to roll back the heavy stone at the tomb's entrance. But when they arrived — wonder of wonders! — the stone had been removed and a figure in a dazzling white garment, an angel, was there. Don't be afraid, he told them; go, tell his disciples Jesus has risen. Mary ran back into the city, to the Upper Room where the apostles are gathered, and told them what had happened. The men were skeptical, but Peter and John hurried to the tomb to see for themselves. Finding it empty, they left, not knowing what to think.

From this point, the accounts differ.

John's Gospel tells us that Mary Magdalene followed Peter and John back to the garden and remained there after they left, hoping for some clue to Jesus' whereabouts. Seeing a man she took to be the keeper of the garden, she begged him, "Sir, if you have carried him away, tell me where you have laid him."

"Mary," he replied — and, at once, she knew it was Jesus. She started forward to embrace him, but he told her, "Do not hold me, for I have not yet ascended to the Father; but go to my brethren and say to them, I am ascending to my Father and your Father, to my God and your God."

Again, Mary went running to the apostles, announcing, "I have seen the Lord."

Emmaus

Saint Luke's Gospel records another incident the same day. That afternoon, two men were on the way to Emmaus, situated three hours' walk northwest of Jerusalem. One of them, Cleopas (or Clopas), was the husband of one of the women who had stood with Jesus' mother at the cross. As they walked, sadly discussing the events of recent days, a stranger overtook them and, walking with them, asked what they were talking about.

"About Jesus of Nazareth, a great prophet whom the chief priests and rulers killed," Cleopas replied, adding in surprise, "Are you the only visitor to Jerusalem who does not know the things that have happened there in these days?"

Untroubled, the stranger merely asked another question: "Was it not necessary that the Christ should suffer these things and enter into his glory?" Then, patiently, he showed them from Scripture how Moses and the prophets had foretold what recently had happened. The other two, strangely moved as he spoke, listened intently.

As they neared the outskirts of Emmaus, the stranger seemed of a mind to go on by himself, but Cleopas and his companion urged him to stay with them, and he agreed. Then, at table, he took bread, blessed it, and gave it to them. Suddenly, they recognized Jesus, and he disappeared. "Did not our hearts burn within us," they asked each other, "while he opened to us the Scriptures?"

The men hurried back to Jerusalem to tell the Eleven what had happened. But the apostles had news of their own: "The Lord has risen indeed, and has appeared to Peter." Then Cleopas and his companion recounted their experience on the road to Emmaus, and how they recognized Jesus "in the breaking of the bread."

As they exchanged accounts of these wonders, Jesus himself was suddenly there. "Peace be to you," he told them. To dispel any doubts about whether it was really he, with his own risen body, he asked for and ate a piece of broiled fish. Then he spoke to them much as he had spoken to the men on the road to Emmaus, showing how Scripture foretold his suffering, death, and resurrection. Concluding, he breathed on the apostles and said, "Receive the Holy Spirit. If you forgive the sins of any, they are forgiven; if you retain the sins of any, they are retained."

Thomas the apostle was not with the rest on this occasion, and when the others told him what had happened, he remained unconvinced. "Unless I place my finger in the mark of the nails, and place my hand in his side, I will not believe," Thomas insisted.

After eight days, Jesus appeared again in the Upper Room, and now Thomas was there. After his usual greeting — "Peace be with you" — the Lord turned to the doubting apostle. "Put your finger here, and see my hands; and put out your hand, and place it in my side; do not be faithless, but believing."

"My Lord and my God!" exclaimed Thomas.

"You have believed because you have seen me," Jesus replied. "Blessed are those who have not seen and yet believe."

In Galilee

Jesus instructed the apostles to leave Jerusalem and go to Galilee; so, several days later, they were at the Sea of Galilee, and there Peter announced that he was going fishing. Thomas, Bartholomew, James and John, and two others piled into the boat with him, and off they went. But even after several hours out on the lake, their net remained empty.

Then a man standing on the shore called to them, "Children,

have you any fish?"

"No," was the irritated reply.

"Cast the net on the right side of the boat, and you will find some."

So they cast to the right; at once, the net was so full of fish that they could not even haul it on board.

John cried out, "It is the Lord!"

Hearing that, Peter leaped into the water and swam ashore, while the rest rowed to land dragging the net behind them. When they landed and counted the fish, they found one hundred and fifty-three of them — large ones, too, although the net was not broken.

Jesus had a charcoal fire going on the beach, with fish already on it and bread warming beside it, so they added several of the newly caught fish and broiled them too. "Come and have breakfast," he told them, handing around the food.

When breakfast was over, Christ drew Peter aside, and as they walked together along the shore, he asked, "Simon, son of John, do you love me more than these?"

"Yes, Lord," Peter answered, "you know that I love you."

"Feed my lambs," Jesus told him. Several moments passed. Then: "Simon, son of John, do you love me?"

"Yes, Lord, you know that I love you."

"Tend my sheep." Another pause. Then a third time: "Do you love me?"

Troubled by the repetition, Peter said, "Lord, you know everything; you know that I love you." Then it dawned on him that Jesus was reminding him, gently but pointedly, of his triple denial, while inviting him to renew his declaration of fidelity and love.

Now Jesus was speaking again, telling Peter what to expect in his role as Christ's vicar and the head of the Church. "Feed my sheep," he repeated, and then: "Truly, truly, I say to you, when you were young, you fastened your own belt and walked where you would; but when you are old, you will stretch out your hands, and another will fasten a belt for you and carry you where you do not wish to go."

Glancing back, Peter saw John not far behind them. "Lord, what about this man?" he asked.

Never mind about him, Jesus answered: "Follow me."

Soon after that encounter at the lake — according to tradition, forty days after the Resurrection — Jesus led the apostles and other disciples to a mountain in Galilee and there told them: "All authority in heaven and on earth has been given to me. Go therefore and make disciples of all nations, baptizing them in the name of the Father and of the Son and of the Holy Spirit, teaching them to observe all that I have commanded you; and behold, I am with you always, to the close of the age."

Then Jesus ascended to heaven, while his followers set out to do as he had said.

Scripture

Matthew 28:1–10, 16–20
Mark 16:1–8
Luke 24:13–35
John 20:1–29; 21:1–23

Works Consulted

The translation of the Gospels used in this book is the Revised Standard Version, Second Catholic Edition, as found in *The Ignatius Catholic Study Bible, The New Testament* (Ignatius Press). The same volume's introduction, commentary, and notes by Scott Hahn and Curtis Mitch have also been of much help, as were its maps by David Notley. At various points (noted in the text) I have also drawn on the *Catechism of the Catholic Church* for interpretative comments.

Other works consulted are:

Richard Bauckham, *Jesus and the Eyewitnesses: The Gospels as Eyewitness Testimony* (Eerdmans)

John A. Beck, *The Holy Land for Christian Travelers* (Baker Books)

G. K. Chesterton, *The Everlasting Man* (Doubleday Image)

Henri Daniel-Rops, *Daily Life in the Time of Jesus* (Hawthorn)

St. Josemaría Escrivá de Balaguer, *Christ Is Passing By* (Scepter)

Germain G. Grisez, *The Way of the Lord Jesus*, Volume One; *Christian Moral Principles* (Franciscan Herald)

Romano Guardini, *Meditations on the Christ* (Sophia Institute); *The Lord* (Regnery)

Leroy A. Huizenga, *Behold the Christ: The Gospel of Matthew* (Emmaus Road)

Larry W. Hurtado, *Lord Jesus Christ: Devotion to Jesus in Earliest Christianity* (Eerdmans)

R. A. Knox, trans., *The New Testament of Our Lord and Saviour Jesus Christ* (Sheed & Ward)

John P. Meier, *A Marginal Jew: Rethinking the Historical Jesus* (Doubleday)

The Navarre Bible New Testament, Compact Edition (Scepter)

St. John Henry Newman, *Parochial and Plain Sermons* (Ignatius)

Fulton Oursler, *The Greatest Story Ever Told* (Doubleday Image)

Michael Pakaluk, *The Memoirs of Peter* (Regnery)

Joseph Ratzinger, *Introduction to Christianity* (Crossroad)

Joseph Ratzinger/Pope Benedict XVI, *Jesus of Nazareth: The Infancy Narratives* (Image); *Jesus of Nazareth: From the Baptism in the Jordan to the Transfiguration* (Doubleday); *Jesus of Nazareth: Holy Week: From the Entrance into Jerusalem to the Resurrection* (Ignatius)

Edward Sri, *God with Us* (Emmaus Road)

Thomas G. Weinandy, OFM Cap, *Jesus Becoming Jesus: A Theological Interpretation of the Synoptic Gospels* (Catholic University of America)

About the Author

Russell Shaw holds BA and MA degrees from Georgetown University. From 1957 to 1966 he was a reporter with the Catholic News Service and from 1966 to 1969 director of publications and information of the National Catholic Educational Association. Shaw served as Secretary for Public Affairs of the National Conference of Catholic Bishops/United States Catholic Conference (now the U.S. Conference of Catholic Bishops) from 1969 to 1987 and as director of information of the Knights of Columbus from 1987 to 1997. He is contributing editor of *Our Sunday Visitor* weekly. *The Life of Jesus Christ* is his twenty-fourth book. Others include *Nothing to Hide* (2008), *American Church* (2013), and *Eight Popes and the Crisis of Modernity* (2016). The Catholic University of America awarded him an honorary Doctorate of Humane Letters in 2019. He and his wife, Carmen, have five children, ten grandchildren, and two great-grandchildren.